MARKETING IN ACTION SERIES

AN INTRODUCTION TO INTERNATIONAL MARKETING

A Guide to Going Global

KEITH LEWIS AND MATTHEW HOUSDEN

KOGAN PAGE

Dedication

To Pop

MJH

To Jan

KL

YOURS TO HAVE AND TO HOLD

BUT NOT TO COPY

Kogan Page Limited
120 Pentonville Road
London N1 9JN

British Library Cataloguing in Publication Data

A CIP record for this book is available from the British Library.

ISBN 0 7494 2246 7

Typeset by JS Typesetting, Wellingborough, Northants.
Printed and bound by Biddles Ltd, Guildford and Kings Lynn.

Contents

Acknowledgements

The authors would like to thank all those connected with the publication of this book.

A special thanks to Joanne Lindsay and to Phil Holden for their work on Chapters 11 and 12 respectively.

Thanks too are due to the many students at the University of Greenwich, the CIM and the IDM, whose experiences have been shared with the authors and whose input is an inevitable part of the whole book.

Thanks also to Britt Howell for her help with the manuscript.

Finally, and most importantly, thanks are due to our partners, Jan Lewis and Katherine Housden, for their unfailing support and encouragement.

1

Why all Businesses Need to Think International

INTRODUCTION

Everybody is talking about globalization. Globalization drives government policy and it informs the strategies of major corporations. The 1997 merger plans of Guinness and Grand Metropolitan to create a single global player in the spirits business – Diageo – and the recent attempted merger of BT and MCI to create Concert, a global telecommunications organization, reflect this. Globalization influences all our lives.

Consider the following scenario: you wake up in the Hilton hotel to the sound of a Sony radio alarm. You turn on the Toshiba television and tune into CNN for the world news. The latest merger in the pharmaceuticals sector is the lead story; already shares in the sector have risen in all major markets. The second story involves a 20 point increase in the FTSE index in response to a rise on Wall Street; the Hang Seng is expected to follow suit. You call into the office via your Nokia cellphone and leave voicemail for your colleagues in the US, Asia Pacific and Europe regions. You will see them later at the scheduled videoconference. You call room service and order your usual Del Monte Fruit Juice, Kellogg's Cornflakes and Nescafé. You get dressed, putting on your Armani suit. Picking up your Louis Vuitton briefcase you leave the room and head out into the streets, already teeming with cars made by Ford, Nissan and BMW. The City feels alive and vibrant – you love doing business in . . .

You could be in virtually any major city in the world ready to meet customers from any place. Globalization affects us all as customers, and therefore has an impact on every business.

Globalization cannot be just the concern of government or the mega-corporation. Every day small companies are creating global networks of customers using the latest technology to bridge geographic and cultural barriers. If your business is not out there working to exploit these opportunities, then you can be sure that your competitors will be. More importantly, international operators are already looking at the value of your domestic customers. The competitor from hell is just around the corner.

THE SHAPE OF THINGS TO COME: MAKING SENSE OF THE NEW WORLD ORDER

Technology

The four fastest growing companies in the UK are in telecommunications; the pace of change is staggering. There is more computing power in the average family car than there was in the Apollo 11 spacecraft that landed on the Moon. The only limit to the application of IT appears to be imagination.

The price of today's average desktop personal computer is £1,000, and some are already available for just £500. In 1970 a similar machine would have cost £1 million. In 1970 the cost of hiring a new graduate was £1,500, but in 1998 it is £16,000. Computers, with their huge processing capability, are now far cheaper than people and the differential is widening. All companies now have access to technology, and when it is used creatively small companies can compete directly with the major players in the global market. As the power of computers increases, so their cost continues to fall. This will continue to have huge implications for the way businesses of all sizes configure themselves to produce value for the customer. Technology is changing the way that all businesses are doing business and is opening global markets to the smallest of companies.

Global networks

In the 1950s Marshall McLuhan talked about the global village. In 1998 it has happened. We have instant access to news about our 'neighbours' in Australia and world-wide via CNN and satellite channels. It has been said that the average British adult knows as much about Californian culture, through programmes such as *Baywatch*, (the world's most viewed TV programme) as about his or her native culture. We visit our neighbours more often than ever before. Tourism is the world's largest business. We provide for our needs in the global shopping malls on the Internet and via QVC and other international shopping channels. We can find partners or talk with potential partners anywhere in the world. The world's first Internet wedding recently took place. We can gamble on the 4.45 horse race at Epsom, watch the race and lose our shirts at the same time in betting shops in London, Singapore and Tokyo.

Telecommunications costs are also plummeting, and this enables (among many other things) doctors in the USA to process prescriptions and patient records in Bangalore at one thirtieth of the total cost of employing a practice secretary and doing the task in Philadelphia. British Airways' ticketing is handled in Mumbai (Bombay). Any information-based process can be handled anywhere. For example, at present the Royal Mail's Mount Pleasant sorting office in London covers an area the size of 14 football pitches in a prime residential and business district. Technology plays a major part in sorting mail. All those letters for which the postcode cannot be recognized by optical character recognition (OCR) are photographed and the images transferred to a screen in an air-conditioned room. In this room hundreds of people read and key in the postcodes, which are then recorded as series of dots on the envelopes themselves. They process 30,000 letters an hour in this way. However, there is no reason why this has to be done in central London. Coding could be done on Mount Rushmore or even at the top of Mount Everest if it were desirable. The production line in many product sectors can be dispersed globally, with elements of physical production glued together by a combination of information technology and global logistics. FedEx is one of the world's largest airlines, yet transports only goods.

'Virtual' products for global markets can be created by a global 'virtual' organization. Production, delivery and consumption can exist together or separately depending on the requirements of customers and the needs of the organization.

'Knowledge itself is power', said Francis Bacon in 1516. Today companies have access to more information than ever before, and this is enabling sensitive activity in the global market-place. The problem of information overload is in itself being dealt with by technology. Intelligent Web browsers can be trained to filter out irrelevant data. Market Information Systems are reinvented as Decision Support Systems, indicating not just an array of data but the range of decisions the data supports.

As manufacturers take more power from their intermediaries, using technology and improvements in logistics to deal with their global customers direct, so they learn more about those customers and their *individual* needs. Technology now allows products to be designed for individuals without consequent reduction in margins. Henry Ford once said 'People can have the Model T in any colour – so long as it's black'. Now Ford, a global corporation, are close to saying 'any car you like – period'. The 'one to one future', as described by Peppers and Rogers (1993) in their book of the same name, is here today.

Customers' affluence: the convergence of needs, the triumph of the individual

As customers are faced with a convergence in the information, which they use to make decisions, so their needs are becoming increasingly similar. Countries which 20 years ago were described as economic 'basket cases' are now competing with the 'giants' of the West. Conversely, Korean companies relocate to Southern Wales partly because it is cheaper to employ a British worker than the equivalent in Korea.

As the Eastern bloc has fragmented and the Cold War market has disappeared, Western governments and businesses are focusing on the drive to develop markets in the Far East, and are busy opening factories to supply the newly emerging demand.

Certainly, living standards are rising virtually everywhere in the world. India now has the world's largest 'middle class', a relative term, but indicative of progress of a sort. Microsoft's Bill Gates's recent visit to India was not for a vacation, but was symbolic of Microsoft's recognition that India will soon be the world's largest market for PCs. That China will ultimately take over appears to be a matter of time, not speculation.

Once nations reach a certain level of GDP per capita (around $15,000 according to Kenichi Ohmae, 1989), cultural differences while, still important, appear to become more easily subjugated to commercialism and consumerism. If the rich are getting richer, so are the poor (albeit at a slower rate). When Tom Peters (1994) says we have the ability to reinvent the planet, what he means is that we can reinvent the planet in the American way.

China's coastal region houses 300 million people. Many of these people are expressing themselves through the purchase of a wide variety of consumer and luxury products in a fashion that would have been unimaginable 20 years ago. A revolution in culture is taking place as the Chinese are allowed to explore and rediscover a mercantile tradition.

It is estimated that there will be five million Chinese tourists travelling overseas within the next three years. They will further fuel moves towards economic liberalization, taking images of western affluence to the heart of Chinese society and contributing to the process of globalization.

Throughout Asia the progress is staggering. Contrast a vision for the future of the United Kingdom which consisted of putting 3000 extra policemen on the streets (John Major at a Conservative Party Conference) with a vision for the future for Malaysia which aims to double living standards in 20 years. Singapore is now Mercedes-Benz's second largest market per capita in the world, Germany being the first.

This is a universal phenomenon. Twenty years ago a trip to Benidorm was a luxury for most Britons. Today we are travelling to Bali for summer holidays and a round the world trip can be bought for under £1000.

As we travel, global corporations meet our needs. The world's most recognized symbols are not the Crescent or the Cross but McDonald's Golden Arches, closely followed by the Nike Swoosh. These brand names and symbols are major global assets and are universally recognized. The major problem of litter in the Himalayas is created from Coke bottles and Nabisco biscuit wrappers.

The American dream is global. Coca-Cola's mission statement stresses the company's desire to put a bottle of Coke within arm's reach of every person in the world, closely followed by the recognition that Coke's competition is tap water – which Coca-Cola aims to replace as the major drinking fluid. The Académie Française rails against the increasing use of Americanisms in the French language, but it is like the Dutch boy with his finger in the dyke: Le Big Mac and particularly L'Internet are here to stay. In order to preserve the integrity of the language, the Académie would need to adopt the policy of the Taliban in Afghanistan, cutting off all contact with the outside world.

Global companies can create the brand identity that their customers require. The country of origin is becoming less important in the buying decision. Some Waterford crystal is made in Hungary. Berghaus jackets are made in northern England, not Norway. A French company owns HP Sauce. Volkswagen Polos are produced in a Skoda plant in the Czech Republic. Global companies can leverage all the benefits of economies of scale, but still project a domestic focus if their customers require it – 'Insiderisation' as Ohmae (1989) calls it.

Affluence creates demand and has created an unprecedented response by companies. We are faced with an unbelievable range of choices. The produce of the world is brought to our doorsteps: Kenyan beans, Chilean wines, Jamaican coffee and Dutch flowers (actually flown from South America) are available in your local supermarket daily. As we become more sophisticated in our purchasing behaviour so global markets fragment, and this presents an ongoing opportunity for all companies. Globalization cannot mean homogenization. This goes against all the basic philosophy of marketing. What international companies can do is to create and combine 'packages' of satisfactions for individual customers. Indeed, in many maturing markets customers reject choice. They want only what they want. They don't want a choice of package holidays; they want to create their own experience. National bicycles, a leading Asian producer, has the capability of producing 11,000,000 variants of its basic model.

Competition and collaboration: the global snakepit

As consumer demands converge and assume global characteristics, so the competitive domain has internationalized. Regionalization, the creation of trading blocs and the deregulation/liberalization of trade have helped this. There is no such thing as a national market. British markets are, at the very least, European, and the long-term plans for the expansion of the EU may mean a single market stretching from Vigo (Portugal) to Vladivostok (the extreme Eastern border of Russia). All companies need to consider the international aspect of their competitive environment.

The Korean cutlery sector produces, ships, distributes and sells its products in the UK more cheaply than a Sheffield cutlery manufacturer can purchase the steel from a mill five miles away.

The message is clear: unless value is added through marketing there is little future. We must either produce there or be special here. No company can feel secure in its domestic market unless it enjoys government protection, which offends EU rules and the World Trade Organisation (WTO). The tide of the state has rolled back and has left unprepared companies stranded in the heat of international competition. This is unlikely to change under future governments.

Local markets are global markets. If local markets can be defined as those within six hours' flying time, half the world's population lies within six hours of Hong Kong.

Companies must be aware that the competitor from hell is just around the corner. British motorcycles, British bicycles and British televisions have all suffered: what's to be involved next? Banking and financial services? HKSB (Hong Kong and Shanghai Bank) is the largest company in Britain in terms of market capitalization, yet could easily be threatened and taken over by larger international banks.

As the world of international competition intensifies, companies seeking to create advantages are focusing on core competencies. In order to create the flexibility and add the value that their customers require, they are looking to extend these competencies through the use of collaborative alliances with direct and indirect competitors. Companies will start to combine skills in processes and systems, in operations, and in marketing or branding to create a unique offer. The pace and scale of change mean that companies are finding it hard to go it alone. They therefore seek a common basis upon which advantages can be built and cooperate to achieve their own objectives. Every week one reads of the benefits of strategic alliances.

Ford and Volkswagen/Seat produce a common chassis for their multi-purpose vehicles (people carriers) in Portugal. The Galaxy (Ford), Sharon (VW) and Alhambra (Seat) are all basically identical, but are branded differently. They compete on non-product values, eg servicing, brand image and corporate heritage.

While acquisition is an alternative route to success, it is often recognized that the damage done in the process is not worth it.

Global networks and standards have infiltrated every aspect of commercial and personal life. Microsoft's software runs on 90 per cent of the world's PCs and is shaping the future of communication and business processes. Telecommunication networks are similarly configured. Collaboration exists, in that the network is shared, but companies compete to provide local access and in the development of added value and customized services. This is increasingly the way forward for companies in many sectors. Most companies cannot today afford to invest in R&D in systems that will not be standard world-wide. Bateaux and Apple are just two examples of the problems of going it alone.

Money and government

Money is the driver of this process. Global money markets exist to create the best returns anywhere in the world. Trillions of dollars are traded daily on the global casino in the search for the micro-changes in rates that yield billions of dollars of profit. Black Wednesday (the day the UK left the European Exchange Rate Mechanism) showed the folly of defining a national economic policy that was dislocated from the regional policy. Governments are simply two-bit players in this global casino – they can haul on the tiller of the national economy and produce barely any change in the overall direction of the global market. Control of macroeconomic policy is shifting away from governments, and the concept of nation means little against the concept of corporation. Governments are currently constrained by borders, whereas corporations span the globe.

Companies can raise money worldwide and international corporations are accountable to shareholders world-wide. Accountability to national governments is secondary to this key relationship. The ceding of control of interest rates in the UK to the Bank of England is an example of the need to recognize international realities and the relative powerlessness of government to really control international events.

THE SHAPE OF THINGS TO COME: YOUR COMPANY IN THE NEW WORLD ORDER

The traditional processes for assisting an organization in the development of its expansion into international markets are well documented. You can read about them in many books on international marketing. They provide the novice with an insight into internationalization with security. They provide comfort to the inexperienced international manager.

The problem is that they represent a set of rules, a toolkit if you like. But in reality they are not especially helpful in ensuring that the organization is sufficiently differentiated from competitors in the eyes of potential customers.

In a complex and fast-moving international environment the traditional planning models become a sandpit for an ostrich – they represent little more than adequate reporting systems. Benchmarking can produce and confirm mediocrity. Research reports on history and explains the past. What's more, since virtually every company competing in a market sector uses the same research methods, they all too often end up producing 'me-too' identikit products – safe yet dull.

What matters is not the process itself but the quality and originality of the thinking within these formulaic structures and the ability of the organization to respond to the changes taking place, both in the global environment and (particularly) in the minds of customers. This is what creates real advantage – not the fact that we have developed a SWOT analysis from information to which most of our competitors also have access.

How do we respond to the environment for international business outlined above? How do we, as Hamel and Prahalad (1994) say, 'compete for the future', in international markets? Set out below are some important, challenging guidelines for the future.

Stop playing by your local industry rules – be different!

▪ Step outside the industry loop; look at your industry from your customers' point of view. What values are they buying into?
▪ Invent your industry's future in partnership with your customers.
▪ Involve your customers in the development of your strategy. Create the strategy around the customer's own values.

Here are some examples:

▪ Swatch reinvented the watch market.
▪ Renault reinvented the car with the Espace.
▪ Alcopops reinvented the drinks market.
▪ First Direct has changed banking forever.

Are you capable of challenging orthodoxy? Who will reshape or reinvent your industry? Will it be you or will you abdicate this to your competitors?

▪ Create the future for your organization – or fade away.
▪ Follow and lead your customers – interact
▪ Create needs, then surpass expectations.

- Delight your customers. Excite them. Challenge their view of the future.
- Test new ideas constantly.
- Let customers create their own value. Encourage complaints. Don't dictate – communicate.
- Innovate or die – the Ozymandias syndrome
- Recognize that today's success is tomorrow's failure.
- Create a culture that challenges orthodoxy.
- What is your innovation rate? Set objectives for innovation. Demand innovation.
- Recognize obsolescence in the planning cycle. Plan the demise of products/services.
- If it ain't broke. . . break it!

Internationalize the operation

- Remove external barriers – create the virtual organization.
- Seek partnerships outside national boundaries with suppliers, with facilitators and essentially with customers.
- Learn internationally.

Take risks

- Be first to market.
- Add value through cooperation – trust your partners.
- Use alliances: create supplier/customer networks

Create an intelligent organization

- Learn from everything. Real difference comes from applying different data and using a different mind set. A good example appeared in an announcement in the *Wall Street Journal* that St Jo (an abbreviation for a major US producer of paper) had recently appointed a new CEO from the Walt Disney Corp. Why would a paper maker seek leadership from a world class entertainment company? The explanation is simple if you can think 'outside the box':
  - Paper comes from trees.
  - Trees grow on land.
  - St Jo owns vast tracts of land in Florida.
  - Disney adds enormous value to land by creating theme parks. St Jo has all the expertise it could ever need to make paper –

what it is seeking is a new innovative corporate mindset to leverage under-utilized assets.

■ Bed learning in the structure and culture of the organization.
■ Information is not enough – it must be accessible and acted upon.
■ Create an effective learning organization.
■ Capitalize on and leverage this learning.
■ Think differently. Create differentiation!

People create organizations

■ Aspirational leadership creates inspirational people.
■ Employ those with an international outlook.
■ Employ the best, not the cheapest.
■ Train everybody to be customer-focused.
■ Communicate – in networks, in learning groups, with suppliers, with customers, with competitors.

Understand customers

Ultimately, technology, international finance, governments and competitors can fade away. What matters today, and what has always driven business, is customers. If we can meet our customers' needs better than our competitors then we will thrive; if not, we will fail.

This requirement in international markets is not easy. What we hope to do in this book is to develop an innovative, actionable approach to international planning. We will challenge preconceived ideas that have little relevance to the contemporary and future world without dispensing with the key disciplines that need to inform business activity. Some of what we suggest might at times seem odd, even bizarre. That is our intention. We want to provoke some controversy and make you think.

We believe that internationalization is an imperative for survival in almost every business and a prerequisite for any organization to thrive.

Let's go to work.

SUMMARY

Globalization is happening; it is driving government policy and is being driven by several factors.

▓ It is creating a new and challenging environment for business.

▓ Information technology is cheaper and more powerful than ever before and will continue to change the way we do business.

▓ It will facilitate and demand the internationalization of all businesses, large or small.

▓ Customers' needs are converging, as the world's population becomes more affluent. Richer customers mean greater profit opportunities.

▓ Customer information needs to be woven into the marketing mix faster and more effectively than ever before.

▓ This challenges the way businesses are organized.

▓ The end of the Cold War means that companies are focusing clearly on the rapidly expanding economies of Asia.

▓ We can no longer count on growth from our mature home markets, and in any case that growth is unlikely to be sufficient to ensure our long-term survival.

▓ Competitive rivalry is intensifying. Many companies are using cooperation and collaboration to meet their individual objectives.

▓ Governments can't help.

Eight rules for shaping the future

▓ Overturn conventional wisdom.
▓ Create partnerships with customers.
▓ Internationalize: think global, act global.
▓ Take risks: make your own luck.
▓ Create the intelligent organization.
▓ Visualize and communicate the future.
▓ Employ the best.
▓ Understand customers.

2

The Route to Market

INTRODUCTION

This is perhaps the most important chapter of the book. We must understand markets, and more importantly the customers who together make up these markets.

This chapter starts to introduce the process of selecting international markets. We must understand the nature of markets: their dynamics and structures. We must understand the range of forces acting on international markets. If we can do this, then as a business we will be in a far better position to evaluate our company's strengths against the opportunities that might be presented. We can begin to classify markets in terms of best to worst potential and target resources accordingly

The haphazard approach

A haphazard approach to international marketing means that some companies, particularly small ones, are dragged into international marketing through, for example, the receipt of unsolicited orders. While these orders are normally welcomed and accepted, they can end up causing problems due to unfamiliarity with export procedure, currency issues, payment methods, invoicing, etc. If these orders then become a platform for the development of international marketing strategy we can begin to compound the difficulties, or at least may be placing valuable and limited resources into a market which might have less potential than other unexplored markets.

The myopic approach

Other companies adopt a supposedly more 'scientific' approach and plan to enter international markets that they believe they know or have some familiarity with.

The corporate battlefield is littered with the corpses of those companies who believed they 'knew' the market. This includes major organizations who have targeted countries they believed to be psychologically 'close' to their home market and invested and failed due to substantial differences in the way that the market operated.

Look at the way companies have targeted the UK market. Anheuser Busch failed to recognize early on that the image of America that was acceptable to the British was not a Beach Boys and Baywatch image but an older image, associated with James Dean and the French Quarter in New Orleans. This is the 'genuine article' as far as America is concerned for the British. Another example is the way that Levi's jeans are advertised and positioned in the jeans market. We can also consider the early problems that EuroDisney experienced through the wholesale export of the US theme park experience into France. The Asterix theme park north of Paris was originally far more acceptable to the French, but now fails to attract the number of foreign visitors that Disneyland Paris (as it is now called) does.

Look at the British experience of marketing in the USA. The thinking is pretty poor but very common: 'I have seen *Star Wars/ West Side Story* – I really understand America. We have a special relationship. I have visited New York. They speak our language'. There are many major companies who have had their fingers burned in the US market. One example is the Pearson Group, who failed to control the distribution network adequately and through a process of discounting on bulk retail purchases were faced with a massive loss. Others include Cadbury, who failed to appreciate the total cost implication of independent activity in the US market and revised their strategy to set up a licensing agreement with Hershey, a major competitor.

These cases represent an eternal problem for any organization embarking on international expansion.

As managers we inevitably view the world from the point of view of our own environment and heritage. This is what James Lee (1966) calls our self-reference criteria (SRC).

SELF-REFERENCE CRITERIA

James Lee, as early as 1966, recognized this unconscious reference to one's own cultural values. It is hard to recognize the impact of SRC, but if you find yourself shouting at a foreign waiter 'Why don't you speak English?', it is clear that something is wrong. In business the influences are more subtle and can be more important. Lee identifies a four-stage approach to help deal with SRC:

1. Define the problem in terms of one's own domestic culture.
2. Define the problem in terms of the foreign culture making no value judgements.
3. Isolate the SRC which affect the problem. How does it complicate the problem?
4. Redefine the problem without SRC.

Sock Shop went bankrupt partly due to the failure to recognize that the format which had worked so well in the UK would not work in the USA. Focusing on opening outlets in the forecourts of railway stations did not work in the USA. Railway stations in the USA are generally not places to stop, let alone shop, for the middle income market that Sock Shop targeted.

In our home markets self-reference criteria give us insight and intuition about how customers will respond to our offer, although many middle managers lose touch with even their domestic target market. How many marketing directors read the Sun, despite the fact that most of their customers (up to ten million of them) do?

Of course, in overseas markets customers are a product of their own unique environment. Even if the Americans and the British do share a common language, language is but one expression of a cultural, political and economic framework that influences decision making and buyer behaviour (behavior!). Shaw's description of the USA and the UK as two nations divided by a common language remains true and has never been more accurate. 'Trunk' and 'boot', 'lift' and 'elevator' are well-known examples. You 'wash up' in the USA before dinner; in the UK you 'wash up' after dinner. When an American says she wishes to table a motion she does not want to discuss the issue, but in the UK it would mean that the issue is to be discussed.

Even when great care has been taken to produce an international marketing strategy which avoids the problems of language, other factors can lead to misunderstanding.

Nestlé's advertising of Kit Kat is a good example. An advertisement which used a local language voiceover was used in both Italy and the UK. It showed duck hunters using duck callers and the universal language of ducks, the quack, to attract birds towards their guns. As they look skyward they back into each other, fall over and decide that this represents an ideal opportunity to have a break and, of course, a Kit Kat.

The association with hunting in Italy became more important than the humour that the advertisement was intended to portray, and the snack bar was believed by Italians, who had little experience of the product, to be an expensive luxury confectionery item.

In the next chapter we will look at formal market research and how information can be generated about international marketing opportunities. However, as part of a systematic process towards international development of business we must start to understand how and why overseas markets differ from our own.

THE INTERNATIONAL MARKETING ENVIRONMENT

In this section we consider a framework for the analysis of market opportunities overseas. There are three key areas that businesses must take into account when searching for opportunity:

■ country
■ customers
■ competitors.

Countries

As usual in marketing we have a range of tools to allow us to develop a comparative approach to the analysis of overseas markets. In our home market we should do the same thing, and a situation analysis will be an essential part of the process of marketing planning. This will generally include a Strengths, Weaknesses, Opportunities and Threats (SWOT) analysis, as well as an analysis of the uncontrollable factors operating on the market. Generally this is known as a PEST analysis. Political, Economic, Social and Technical factors will be analysed to establish the extent of their influence on the planning process.

At the level of domestic plans we are generally looking at factors which affect our ability to do business reflecting our broad understanding of the business environment. These may include:

▓ Political: A minor change in business rates
▓ Economic: Inflation rising or falling marginally
▓ Social: The increase in single-parent families
▓ Technical: The growth in telemarketing.

In moving to the international scene we are generally looking at broader indicators that may show greater or lesser potential for activity, ie the process of evaluating and ranking opportunity. There are several mnemonics available to describe the process that we must go through as we begin to assess international markets:

▓ SLEPT includes legal systems
▓ PLESTIE + C includes industrial, environmental or Green issues and competitive analysis
▓ STEEPLE ignores the competitive domain and industry structures, but adds an ethical audit.

If you can think for yourself you should not need to have recourse to these devices, but should simply recognize that what is required is an analysis of those factors that will have an impact on the potential profitability of your business – a task which may include all or some of the above factors, but which may also include other areas, for example currency or the role of public institutions. This process will need to be reviewed, as the appropriate analytical frameworks will change over time as the key success factors for business themselves change.

For example, ethics and the environment have emerged as key factors in certain industry sectors, with certain organizations basing profitable business on ethical or environmental foundations; equally, some organizations are losing business because of a lack of attention to these factors. Body Shop has created a multi-million pound international business by positioning body care products on an ethical/environmental platform. 'Not tested on animals' provides the business with a unique and sustainable advantage. The oil industry, however, finds its activities monitored at every turn by environmental pressure groups which, in their own way, have created substantial international businesses. Shell recently announced a committment to 'ethical' business, a response to ongoing adverse publicity surrounding their operations.

How to construct a business environment (PEST) analysis

Too often business pays lip service to this process. It becomes a rote activity, and information is presented in the business plan with no interpretation or analysis. The data must be considered against the business's ability to impact and relate to the market – to your customers. You should work out an analysis of factors relevant to your own business (Figure 2.1).

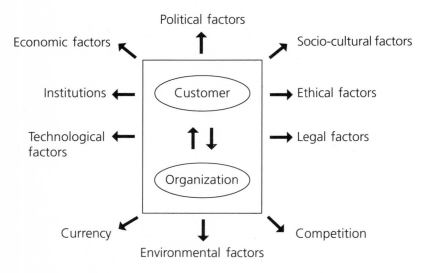

Figure 2.1 *Managing the marketing environment*

At a broad level some factors will be consistent across most sectors: for example political stability, competitive intensity or social cohesion.

Usefully, Phillips, Doole and Lowe (1994) have developed a comprehensive model encompassing environmental analysis within a 12C framework. These include:

1. Country: basic PEST analysis
2. Choices: which country offers the greatest potential
3. Concentration: geographic spread, market structures
4. Culture: what socio-cultural factors will impact on our ability to do business
5. Consumption: market size and dynamics
6. Capacity to pay: the ability of customers to pay for our product
7. Currency: how stable is the currency? To what risk are we exposed by carrying on business in a particular country?

8. Channels of distribution: are channels available to get our product to market?
9. Commitment: the ability to exploit the market
10. Communications: the ability to reach our target audience
11. Contractual obligations: legal frameworks
12. Caveats: other factors to be aware of

Whatever framework is selected it is important that the analysis should contain a predictive/forecasting element. Let's look at just one of these elements – the 'P' of PEST.

POLITICAL FACTORS

If we agree that the EU should now be considered as a home market, what is the future of the EU and how will it influence our ability to do business in Europe? There are several scenarios we may choose to consider. Will Europe be:

1. Competitive Europe, in which
   (a) Market forces predominate within a minimal legislative framework.
   (b) Mergers and acquisitions take place without referral.
   (c) State support for businesses is removed, no farm subsidies.
   (d) Private welfare replaces public welfare.
2. Conscience Europe, in which
   (a) Social/environmental factors are key influences on the business environment.
   (b) A high tax Europe with further consideration for workers' rights.
   (c) State support available for personal and business needs.
3. Cluster Europe, in which
   (a) Provision will be made for local variation through legislation.
   (b) There is a continuing role for social regeneration funding alongside allowance for exchange rate fluctuation in peripheral economies.

Other considerations include:

▓ The widening or deepening of Europe.
▓ The role of national and regional identity.
▓ Relationships with other trading blocs.

There is a hierarchical and systematic approach to the analysis of PEST factors. As we start to scan international markets we set criteria at the broadest level against which we can assess opportunity. At this level our general knowledge can be useful, particularly when allied to common sense.

For example, if we are selling central heating systems or ski wear we can immediately rule out countries with an equatorial or tropical climate. We may require that we do business with countries which have a convertible currency; this will again rule out certain countries.

Majaro suggests a useful approach to this screening process (Figure 2.2).

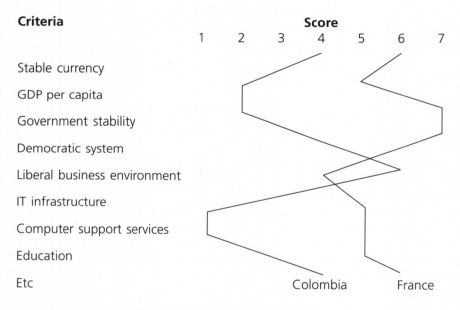

Figure 2.2 *The screening process*

The principle is clear. Criteria are selected according to our judgement of key success factors. We can then rank countries against selected criteria to ensure that the ongoing process of evaluation focuses on those markets which have potential.

We can exclude markets on the basis of this assessment. If resources are scarce, then the average score at which we deselect countries can be higher. This means that more countries will be excluded at this early stage and less money will be spent at the next level.

Information is derived from a variety of sources, and at this preliminary screening government statistical offices are generally a useful source of data. We discuss this further in the following chapter.

CUSTOMERS

Understanding the customer: the socio-cultural environment

Understanding customers is the principal success factor for any business. In the overseas market one of the keys to understanding is culture. The key to culture is often described as language. This view is true in that the nuances of the spoken or written word can reveal much about the society from which the language has sprung. In understanding cultural norms we can position our product to our advantage. Equally, we can avoid causing offence.

Indeed, the language of subcultures is often used to market products in the home market. Consider the porcelain figures so frequently promoted in the Sunday magazines as 'timeless examples of good taste' and compare this to the language used in the promotion of Tango soft drinks. However, it is clear that language reflects and reinforces culture, which is made up of many different elements, all of which are important.

There has been much recent progress in the area of cultural research, but at this early stage in the process of selecting markets we are concerned with a broad understanding of cultural difference and similarity and the construction of a framework for comparing different cultures. Terpstra (1997) has done this in his book on international marketing. He identifies eight key variables or components of culture. Although the relative importance of these variables may shift, the framework that he suggests is a useful starting point. Detailed analysis of consumer behaviour comes later as we look at market entry and research.

After Terpstra

We should look at all these factors but prioritize research again in relation to the product line and the overall objectives of the business. For example, if we are marketing computer software in business-to-business markets, which are being driven by global technology and international concepts of modernity, then attention to local cultural factors may be less important than in local food and drinks markets.

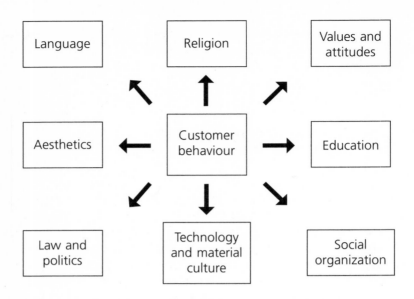

Figure 2.3 *The elements of culture*

Language

Many countries speak more than one language. Belgium has two, Switzerland has four and India has 500, including widely different dialects. Your product might be targeted at a particular language grouping, perhaps reflecting ethnic background and maybe the ability to pay. Translation of the product warranty, instructions for use and all promotional material will almost certainly be required, and this needs great care. It is often not adequate simply to translate into another language. Clichés and turns of phrase that have a deep resonance in certain cultures mean nothing in others. For example, 'it's raining cats and dogs', 'I'm feeling under the weather' and 'He is a smashing bloke' may be misunderstood at best.

Phonetics in brand names may create inappropriate words when combined; Suzuki and Concerto mean to lose everything in China. On the other hand (another problematic phrase!), the beer brand Young's has done well in Mandarin-speaking markets because it sounds the same as the word for virility.

Religious beliefs

Even within the UK, religious beliefs have importance. Recent research from the Policy Studies Institute showed that 73 per cent of the Pakistani community and 76 per cent of the Bangladeshi community rate religion as being very important in the way they live their lives. This contrasted with 30 per cent of Afro-Caribbeans and 11 per cent of the white population. While stated belief often differs from actual behaviour, it is a factor which may influence success in international markets, and in certain markets it may mean the difference between success and failure.

For example, a furore surrounded supermodel Claudia Schiffer's appearance on the catwalk wearing a designer outfit which featured as part of the design words from the Holy Quran offended Muslim beliefs. The former Indian cricket captain Mohammed Azharuddin caused offence by putting his name on Reebok cricket boots. Mohammed and Azhar are both names for the prophet Allah.

Values and attitudes

We can position our product to take advantage of these factors, and we ignore them at our peril. Attitudes to the role of women, decency, and social and business etiquette must be considered. Closing a deal in Japan, for example, will tend to take longer than in Europe or the USA, and will certainly involve far more face-to-face contact, at various levels of seniority. Attitudes to social behaviour vary, and refusing to drink vodka during informal meetings in Eastern Europe may influence the outcome of negotiations.

Education

Levels of education reflect literacy levels and drive the demand for certain products. The market for business training in south-east Asia has been booming fuelled by a generally high level of domestic education infrastructure.

If we are employing local representatives in specialist areas then analysis of general education levels may not reveal sufficient detail. We may need to employ bilingual people with strong IT skills. Research must be appropriate to the objectives of the organization.

Social organization

Who are the key decision makers in families and in businesses? The organization's contact strategy may need to be tailored to meet local needs in this respect.

Research in the UK market shows changing patterns of decision making in the UK. In the past, women were largely excluded from the decision-making process in high-involvement purchases, but today more often women are making decisions about financial services products within the family. In international markets this decision process needs careful research.

An example is the mortgage market in Italy, in which decisions tend to be dealt with within the extended family. This made it very difficult for new entrants into the market. Research showed that an opportunity to communicate about mortgage products emerged when prospective partners visited jewellers to buy their engagement rings. Placing information with jewellers in a marketing alliance has given useful results.

As the role of the extended family may be important in consumer markets, so too in business-to-business markets the configuration of the Decision-Making Unit (DMU) may be more or less centralized.

Technology and material culture

Technology is being adopted at a varying pace. There is a substantial market for IT world-wide, but can this technology be supported? Is there an adequate electricity supply to support IT? Is there a service industry? Can raw materials be obtained for industrial process machinery? The brewing industry in the former Soviet countries is operating below capacity because of the lack of sugar supplies and the non-availability of water.

In many countries the idea of regular servicing of technology needs to be trained into the purchaser.

Law and politics

Legal factors affecting all stages of the process need to be considered. Advice should be taken. Problem areas include agency agreements; in the EU, legislation favours the agent above the principal. Contract and employment law is equally fraught with danger. It does pay to take advice and to stay out of court.

Politics must be considered. Stability and intergovernmental relationships need to be assessed as to their potential impact on international business activity.

Design, aesthetics and branding

There are hundreds of examples of inappropriate design and brand names. Equally, there are examples of inadvertent good practice. Ferrero Rocher succeeded in Hong Kong because of the auspicious gold and red packaging. Equally, British Racing Green, a brand conveying motoring tradition and up-market values, would be unlikely to succeed in China, as green is a colour representing vegetable sellers in Chinese markets. The use of yellow in Brunei is actively discouraged, as it is a Royal colour. New Labour's adoption of the colour purple, representing 'passion' for politics, might have been construed as mourning the death of Old Labour in Mexico.

Examples of brand names with limited export potential include:

▪ Superpiss – a Scandinavian deicer
▪ Pschitt – French Lemonade
▪ Bum Crisps, Bonka Coffee and Bimbo Bread in Spain
▪ Durex sticky-tape in Australia
▪ Smeg electrical appliances in Italy

In Chinese culture the symbol for '8' is lucky, and cars with '8' in the number plate can command a premium in Hong Kong. Conversely, the number four is unlucky; the Alfa Romeo 164 was rebadged as the 168 in Hong Kong.

Competitors

Again the watchword must be what will happen to the competitive situation in the future. Current competition in the local market must be considered, but we must also take account of latent competitors which may be operating in other markets but which have the potential to enter your target market.

Porter's framework for industry analysis is useful for describing the competitive dynamic. Porter (1979) looked at five forces operating within an industry.

1. The threat of new entrants
2. The power of suppliers
3. The power of customers or buyers
4. The threat of substitutes
5. The intensity extent of competitive rivalry

This provides a valuable framework to assess current competition and the threat of competition within industries.

We would extend this framework to include an analysis of competitors':

■ sales and sales trends
■ customers: profiles and motives, levels of satisfaction
■ information management
■ brands
■ products
■ advertising and promotions
■ distribution and sales
■ pricing
■ service levels
■ people
■ financial background
■ management skills
■ asset base.

Information on competitors can be gained via the DTI's market intelligence service or of course by carrying out research via secondary sources or by visiting the market.

It is easy to identify who the competition is, but understanding the basis of their success is more difficult. What is the basis of their position in the market? Are they subject to the same constraints as you in terms of a view on profitability? What will their response be as you enter the market?

SUMMARY

In this chapter we looked at how companies become involved in international marketing and advised against a haphazard or myopic approach. We argue that a planned entry into international markets would yield greater profit and subject the organization to less risk.

We looked at the importance of understanding the nature of markets in the international arena and began to explore the techniques for classifying marketing opportunities. The process of reconciling opportunities now and in the future with the company's ability to exploit these opportunities starts with an understanding of the nature of markets and the customers who make up these markets.

We stressed that managers must be aware of self-reference criteria and should use this awareness to help in the development of international strategy.

A framework for macro analysis was considered. This included looking at countries, customers and the competition.

We looked at the development of SWOT and PEST analyses, recognising that at the preliminary screening stage the factors we analyse are at a broad macro level, but that the nature of this analysis is framed by the organization's objectives in entering international markets.

We looked at the need to understand customer behaviour and the need to deal appropriately with cultural differences that affect the ability to conduct profitable business.

Finally, we looked at the need to assess competitor activity in the market as it exists currently and as it might develop in the future.

3

Getting the Information

INTRODUCTION

There are over 200 countries in the world. To carry out research into all of these would be impossible and impractical, even for major multinational companies. The cost of gathering information and the complexity of analysing diverse data mean that a systematic approach to international market research must be applied.

Those companies looking to export for the first time or looking to extend existing international marketing must ask the following questions.

- Which countries should I target?
- How do I get my product to the market?
- What products are suitable for the market-place?
- How can I most effectively market my products?

For those smaller companies thinking of taking the leap into international marketing or expanding international activity, even the question 'Where to?' may seem daunting. Through general awareness of international markets and competitors we may have a hunch as to which markets might be attractive, but most first-time exporters will have little idea of how to discover and identify appropriate customers, end users or middlemen, how to get products to overseas customers or how best to market those products to customers.

For smaller companies embarking on export marketing for the first time or medium-sized companies considering investing in an overseas sales office, the risks of overseas activity may appear substantial. The cost of gathering even basic information to reduce this risk may seem prohibitive. What we will try to show in this section is that through a systematic approach to information gathering the risks of international marketing can be managed better and that the cost incurred should be seen as an investment in the long-term success of the venture.

We will show that through the use of published data and the range of services in place in the UK to help international marketers, the cost of gathering data need not be prohibitive, especially when assessed against the potential profits available from overseas markets.

WHICH MARKETS: LOOKING FOR OPPORTUNITY OVERSEAS

To begin to narrow the search for suitable overseas markets we can apply screening criteria which filter out countries against established measures of potential. At the earliest stages of screening these criteria may be very broad and based on our judgement and experience as managers. For example:

▪ countries close at hand: European Union; EEA
▪ countries with broadly similar languages: Australia, New Zealand, Canada, USA
▪ countries with broadly similar business culture: Holland, Denmark, Belgium
▪ countries with similarities that are opening up or expanding: South Africa, Singapore, Hong Kong
▪ countries further away, either psychologically or geographically: Taiwan, Japan, Brazil, Venezuela.

As we refine the list of potential markets we can begin to apply increasingly rigorous criteria against which to measure the market's attractiveness. These will include the following.

▪ Accessibility
  – Barriers to entry: tarriffs or non-tarriff barriers
  – International transport and distribution costs: does this make your product uncompetitive in overseas markets?
  – Local distribution and logistics; for example, the ability to export fresh food depends on a refrigerated distribution network.
  – Host government regulations

- Legal restrictions on your product or service or on your ability to market it.
- Home government policy towards trade with a particular nation
■ Customers
- Are products perceived in the same way?
- Are there similarities to our home market?
- Nature of segmentation
- Influences on buying decisions
- Concentration – can we reach sufficient numbers to justify activity?
- Ability to research customers
■ Profitability
- Market size
- Market potential/demand
- Levels of disposable income
- Local tax/other legal requirements
- Repatriation of profits
- Currency risks
- Competition
- Local/other foreign?
- Competitive intensity
- Degree of brand loyalty
- Market sophistication
- Ability to differentiate
- Communications
- Media availability
- Legal restrictions on promotions
- Agency availability
- Sales/promotional practice
- Costs

This is part of a screening process that firms will go through in relation to their product and the markets at which it is targeted. It is clear that as the sophistication of the filtering criteria increases countries will be eliminated. For certain countries this will take place at the very early stages of assessment. The aim of this process is to create a short-list of potential markets which can then be investigated in detail. The extent of this short-list may reflect the overseas potential or the resource base of the company involved. Harrell and Kiefer's model (Figure 3.1) stresses the important connection between company strength and market attractiveness in a nine-cell matrix which helps to prioritize markets.

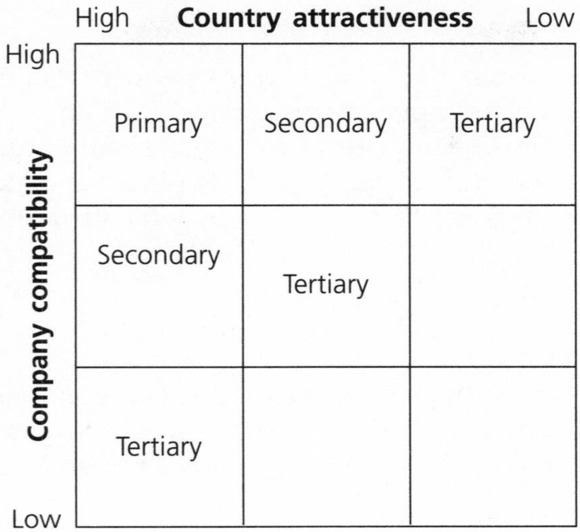

High **Country attractiveness** Low

	High		Low
High	Primary	Secondary	Tertiary
Company compatibility	Secondary	Tertiary	
Low	Tertiary		

Figure 3.1 *Business portfolio matrix (Harrell and Kiefer, 1993)*

The scanning method represents stage one of the process of international marketing research. The next stage is to evaluate the short-list of countries in order to prioritize them. The aim is to look for similarities rather than differences and to cluster those countries which may be approached in similar ways.

Similarities give us opportunities for economies of scale in production and simplification of the international marketing mix, with associated reductions in cost and in management time. These similarities can also allow more rapid development of the company's product in international markets. The company will also be able to apply the experience gained across a wider range of markets and thus gain greater payback on the expenses of establishing an international presence. Sales and profitability can be increased while minimising exposure to risk.

The purpose of the process is to classify markets into categories in order to prioritize international expansion.

Primary markets

These have the highest appeal to the organization in terms of the ability of the organization to invest in the market with the expectation of payback at relatively low risk.

Secondary markets

These markets expose the company to greater risk, but given adequate resources and appropriate caution they are still capable of generating profit. They may be markets that should be addressed in the medium-term future after objectives have been successfully met in primary markets, and with the benefit of the experience gained.

Tertiary markets

Business can be done in these markets, but it is generally opportunistic and incremental, based on low-risk and low-investment strategies. Business will generally be reactive rather than actively sought.

WHAT'S ALREADY AVAILABLE

At first sight the range of information required is daunting. However, much of the information we need is already available and some of this is free, or available at low cost. Researching data which has been published is called secondary or desk research. International desk research does not necessarily have to create insurmountable problems. Indeed, the problems of sourcing secondary data on international markets can be no greater than for the British market. Nevertheless, there are some additional factors that do need to be recognized.

■ Cost: generally, if a charge is made, it will tend to be higher than for information about the UK market, reflecting the difficulties in collating data from international markets.
■ Language: often information will be presented in English. However, when translation is required, back translation is often advisable. Colloquial language needs particular attention. Even when language is supposedly held in common, care needs to be taken. Technical terms also need to be carefully considered. The definition of a 'small' grocery outlet will vary from country to country, even within the EU.
■ Lifestyle segmentation, which may be appropriate in developed markets, is almost always culture-dependent. What do we mean by health food, middle age, leisure activities, family and so on?

Many characteristics of populations are not exportable and will be defined differently.

■ Comparability: we must ensure that when analysing information we are comparing like with like. Problems may include different definitions of markets and the environmental factors which affect them. Social demographics will reflect cultural and economic norms for each country. An example in India: there are 250 million individuals classified as middle class by virtue of relative income. This number exceeds the 'middle class' population of the EU. Definitions of educational attainment and the urban population of a country will vary.

■ Definitions of markets which might appear straightforward can be misleading. For example, is Kit Kat in the biscuit market or the confectionery market?

In some south-east Asian markets, for example, candied fruits are included within the sugar confectionery market.

Definitions will generally reflect the market, and it is often important to take into account these differences.

Even simple measures, which might appear easier to compare meaningfully, need careful thought. For example, measures of GDP per capita can be useful only to a degree. Measures of disposable income which take into account tax regimes, etc., are possibly harder to obtain, but more useful. GDP per capita measures do not reflect the distribution of wealth within a country. Brunei and Saudi Arabia have among the highest GDP per capita in the world; however, most of this is in a few hands.

Market sizes: we must ensure that the market size includes all sectors. For example, data on the food market will often include only the retail market and will exclude the catering and restaurant sector. Market value may be expressed in terms of the retail selling price, whereas we may be interested in the manufacturer's selling price.

In certain markets, the informal trade through street markets may be important and may not be included in official statistics. In other countries there may be a substantial black market operating (for example, that operating currently in dutiable goods between France and the UK). In the export of cigarettes, of the 900 billion cigarettes exported, over 33 per cent 'disappear' (in a puff of smoke). In reality, they re-emerge tax fee at point of sale.

It is clear, as any decent brand manager will tell you, that market size and consequent share can be manipulated. We must be confident in the source and methodology used in gathering this type of data.

■ Time factors: the value of data and information deteriorates over time. International data takes longer to be compiled and disseminated. For example, the latest data comparing research costings in various countries is 1994 based. In the fast emerging and changing markets of south-east Asia, time lag will be crucial and statistical evidence of economic status from official sources will frequently be out of date, as will information on fast-moving technology markets, eg linkages to the Internet or the household penetration of mobile phones.

■ Extent of information: the UK and EU have a substantial and highly sophisticated information-gathering industry. In other markets, this is not the case. This may be due to the economic circumstances or be a result of the information culture that pervades some markets. Generally, Europeans are far more open about their lives and their businesses than south-east Asians. Shareholding structures will also contribute to a culture of openness. However, even in Europe this may be an issue. For example, the Mittelstand companies in Germany tend to be family owned, and attitudes to scrutiny by outsiders, particularly with regard to financial information or other personal information, tend towards non-disclosure.

The way to deal with these problems is as for domestic research: we should, where possible, try to cross-check data from a number of different sources. We should certainly employ a degree of healthy scepticism in dealing with all secondary data. Above all, we need to keep fully informed about our market both at home and abroad, keeping up to date with current affairs and, wherever possible, extending our network of contacts.

DESK RESEARCH SOURCES

Specialist trade press

Most industry sectors will be covered in the trade press. These may be general or highly specialized publications; for example, in the French market the magazine *LSA* covers the grocery trade as a whole, while the magazine *Filiale Farine* looks at the baked goods market.

Quality press, magazines and journals

The general media are another useful source of material. All print media are listed in the very useful publication *The Advertisers Annual*, published by Reed Information Service, East Grinstead.

Trade associations

Trade associations will have varying information provision. Some are excellent, like the Dutch snack food association, which publishes an annual market report; others are less good. Trade associations are listed in the *CBD Directory Of European Trade Associations* or in *Croner's Directory of Marketing Information Sources*.

Directories

Again, a very useful starting point. Among the best known are:

- *Kompass:* lists companies by product group, by country (published by Reed Information Services).
- Euromonitor Directories. Euromonitor publishes a wide range of directories covering market information sources.

Universities

The larger business schools can often provide sophisticated marketing information.

Public libraries

In London: the City Business Library, The Science Reference Library. Many libraries now offer on-line search facilities for a reasonable fee.

Professional bodies

The Chartered Institute of Marketing has a very useful information department which can be used by members, as does the Institute of Direct Marketing.

Chambers of Commerce

While in the UK the Chambers of Commerce do not provide a great information service, in other countries (eg France) the services are very good. Information can be obtained from The Association of International Chambers Of Commerce, Belgrave Square, London.

Your bankers

Any publicly listed company will be subject to scrutiny by the banks. Investor reports can be very useful. Banks will provide a useful service on the mechanics of international marketing.

Electronic media: on-line services, the Internet, CD-ROM

Most services are being made available in electronic format (for example, Mintel is available on CD-ROM). The Internet is a useful source of data. The development of intelligent web browsers has enhanced the capability of the Internet.

International consultancies

For a fee, management or other research consultancies will undertake a study into overseas opportunities. Further information can be obtained from the *Directory of Management Consultancies* and from the Market Research Society.

Syndicated or published research

There is no point in reinventing the research task. Many companies publish reports on overseas markets, including Frost and Sullivan, the Economist Intelligence Unit and Euromonitor.

Findex, from Euromonitor Publications, is a directory of published research and is a useful starting point.

Regional economic groupings

The EU, for example, publishes data on its members through Eurostat. This is now available on the Internet, and further information can be gained from the European Union, Storey's Gate, London.

Other countries' statistical services can be accessed directly or through the DTI's information service (tel: 0171 215 5444). The DTI is an invaluable source of information on overseas markets and a first step is to contact the information desk to see what they can do.

Economic advisory groups

The Organisation for Economic Co-operation and Development (OECD) publishes regular reports on the economic prospects of its members. OECD publications are available through HMSO.

Pressure groups

May be useful as an information source on macro policy (eg Amnesty, Greenpeace).

Competitors' published material

Anything published by a company can yield useful data. This can range from annual reports through to careers literature or specialist sector reports, eg Nestlé's *Hot Beverage Report*. In the international arena, companies may cooperate and exchange top-line data, as both are working within the same constraints and restrictions in terms of information resources.

Development agencies

The United Nations, the World Bank, etc. publish good data on markets at a macro level. Some of this is available on the Internet.

This is not a complete list, but it will give you some guidance. Under each of the above headings it is possible to construct your own tailor-made list of contacts along with the quality and cost of the information they provide.

THE INTERMEDIATE STAGE

Having explored the published sources of data we may have a much greater idea of our potential in an overseas market. There is an intermediate stage between this desk research and full-blown primary research, which we shall call observation. This will be important for 'difficult' markets, where reliable secondary data may be hard to obtain. This intermediate stage includes the following techniques.

■ Visits to the market, both informally or formally through the DTI trade delegations or trade association missions (see below).
■ Visits to exhibitions: these can give valuable information about competitor activity in the market and can lead to good contacts and information.
■ Calls to competitors, suppliers and intermediaries. These might include potential agents or distributors, logistics companies or key players in the overseas markets (identified via the *Kompass* directory).

Other key contacts include your own sources in the industry; colleagues who may have worked in overseas marketing for other companies; and your contacts at computer companies.

This is particularly important for smaller companies, for whom the commissioning of primary research across countries may be prohibitively expensive. Indeed, for some companies this stage may provide the final information upon which entry decisions are made.

PRIMARY RESEARCH

It is perfectly possible for companies to carry out their own market research in overseas markets. For the vast majority, however, the additional skills needed to carry out quantitative studies across markets are not available within the organization. This means that it is advisable to use an agency.

Where to find international market research agencies

■ The Market Research Society directory
■ Recommendations from colleagues or others in your industry sector
■ Past experience
■ Your trade association or Chamber of Commerce

From these contacts a short-list of three or four agencies should be given your research brief.

Who should I choose?

Selection criteria include the following.

▦ Technical capability: languages, computing, transnational networks of researchers, inter-country analysis.
▦ Have they understood the brief?
▦ Have they submitted a creative proposal?
▦ Do they know your business?
▦ Do they have key contacts in overseas markets?
▦ Can you get on with them?

In most developed countries the technical capability to carry out sophisticated quantitative research exists. Sample frames are easily available and a range of agencies exist to facilitate the research task. In some developing or Third World countries, however, the research infrastructure is not as well developed and care must be taken with potential bias.

This bias can relate to skewed samples, reflecting for example the ease of research in urban as opposed to rural areas, or a lack of rigour in the collection of government data.

Bias, however, can occur even in developed countries, for a number of reasons. These include the following.

▦ Geography: in certain countries, access to remote populations may be difficult.
▦ Cultural misunderstandings: difficulties in researching culturally sensitive topics like the role of marriage or family decision making.
▦ Cultural diversity within countries: the ethnic composition of nations.
▦ Economic divergence within nations.
▦ Language problems relate to linguistic pluralism within countries; this highlights the need to undertake back translation of questionnaires, etc.
▦ The ability to understand and interpret culturally determined concepts (eg after dinner mints, leisure time, the family).
▦ Infrastructure constraints on the ability to conduct certain research methodologies (eg telephone ownership, the nature of postal services).

The best research agencies will be able to suggest ways of overcoming these problems and will have the staff in place to counter potential cultural bias.

Government assistance

The UK Government offers a number of services to help exporters. The export marketing research scheme will offer free professional advice and financial help to small and medium-sized businesses. The DTI will fund up to 50 per cent of the cost of any approved project up to £20,000. Research proposals are assessed by the Association of British Chambers Of Commerce (tel: 01203 694 484).

The DTI also runs a Market Information Enquiry service which provides basic research through the commercial departments of embassies overseas. Details are available via the DTI (tel: 0171 215 5444).

Conclusion

Good information increases the chances of success in international marketing and reduces the associated risk. International research is often time-consuming and may be expensive for the smaller firm. We need to think about the Pareto effect: we cannot know everything about potential overseas markets, but we need to know enough. We must be rigorous and disciplined in our approach to information gathering, setting research objectives around key information required and planning how this will be obtained.

- What are our objectives as an organization?
- What critical information do we need?
- Where will we find this information?
- How long will it take to gather the data?
- How much will it cost?
- Who will carry out this work?
- What do we intend to do with this information?
- What are the full implications of inaccurate or incomplete data?

In taking international decisions some information is better than no information, and second guessing in overseas markets is difficult.

SUMMARY

Much of the information required to support international marketing activity is available within the UK either at no charge or at least very cheaply. A number of sources are indicated throughout the chapter.

Primary research can be replaced by the intermediate stage, which involves informal primary research via electronic media and visits to the markets in question.

Primary research can be carried out overseas by companies themselves, but is more usually done through international research agencies. The DTI may support this research work.

4

Planning for International Markets

INTRODUCTION: PLANNING ORDER FROM CHAOS

The increasing complexity of the international environment means that many business gurus are beginning to rethink the value of traditional planning frameworks. They have seen that the process of planning in many organizations is a laborious and uninspired task, which *has* to be completed.

Tom Peters asks businesses to adopt 'Crazy Ways For Crazy Days', and he has a point. As we described earlier, the pace of change in international marketing is mind-blowing and the amount of information about international markets is staggering. Rather than using planning to deliver the insight and discipline to enable profitable business activity, simply completing the planning process becomes a goal in itself for many companies.

In international markets, planning and control are vital to inform day-to-day operation and the development of sustainable long-term strategic direction for any organization. In addition, plans must be flexible enough to deal with the uncertainty that is an inevitable part of business in international marketing.

For smaller companies this is not so important. It is possible to 'muddle by' in our home markets simply because we are familiar with the market and can react to situations as they occur. In overseas markets, small companies can fail to react to problems and, equally importantly, be unprepared for successes. Success can play havoc with cash flows and production planning. Companies have been known to fail with full order books.

Planning provides a structure and approach to 'activity'. It is not a solution in itself, but helps organizations to reach solutions to business problems.

There is no packaged international marketing solution or approach to planning. What works for one company may or may not work for another. Certainty is not a raw ingredient of marketing. We require a framework that embraces and accepts uncertainty and which provides companies with a means of incorporating uncertainty into plans for growth.

THE INTERNATIONAL DIMENSION

We are familiar with the planning process in the local market, which reflects our local culture. We are at ease with a customer base with which we are familiar and in which self-reference criteria help rather than hinder the planning process. The international dimension adds to the complexity of the planning process.

International planning will involve:

▓ many markets
▓ many languages
▓ different cultural drivers influencing consumer choice and behaviour
▓ different currencies and transactional cultures
▓ widely differing levels of marketing support services
▓ scarce, expensive or unobtainable information
▓ unstable financial regimes
▓ unstable political regimes
▓ restrictive trade practices
▓ legal constraints on formal business practice
▓ different informal business etiquette
▓ different competitive environment
▓ prejudice on both sides
▓ different interpretation of market segments
▓ different product use
▓ counterfeiting, smuggling, grey/unofficial markets
▓ parallel importing.

The international marketing planning framework

This framework identifies four levels of decision making. Dealing with the key components of the planning framework is essential for success in international marketing.

Stimuli

Companies enter the international market for a variety of reasons and in response to a number of different stimuli. These include:

- responding to casual orders
- information derived from informal information sources
- the enthusiasm of management for international travel!
- the enthusiasm of management for corporate growth
- proximity to raw materials: labour, materials, technology or money
- following home customers as they expand overseas
- competitor response
- retaliation against companies entering the home market.

The number of stimuli is obviously greater than this list. The important thing is that the decision should emerge from the formal corporate planning process, or if it doesn't that the decision is formally developed within an operating framework. The ability to generate ideas is different from the ability to make money from them.

Decision to go international

This has to have the backing of the senior managers in the company. The development of international business is not a tactical bolt-on to domestic marketing. It will impact on every area of the business, and the whole business must be geared up to deal with the pressures that an increased level of international activity will generate. All aspects of the business function – production, operations, finance, human resources and marketing – will be involved. 'International' must be enshrined in the mission statement of the business and supported from the top.

Corporate objectives should encompass the full impact of international marketing. International activity may be used to generate short-term benefit, but in all truth appropriate long-term involvement should be imperative if the firm is to engage in a serious dialogue with overseas customers. This may involve a short-term fall in profitability in order to fund a patient and long-term commitment which will ultimately improve profitability.

Figure 4.1 *The international marketing planning framework*

Country information

The macro-level PEST factors considered in Chapter 2 need to be assessed at this stage, and they should be set against the ability of the company to carry on business in overseas markets.

Company information

Company strengths and weakness in relation to a broad overseas strategy should be analysed at this stage. This does not just mean identifying the components of a general SWOT, but should involve critically evaluating the company's capability and compatibility with the demands of international marketing. The factors to be considered include:

■ management, motivation and enthusiasm
■ financial stability
■ management skills
■ administrative capability
■ operational capability
■ production capacity
■ expertise in export systems
■ access to facilitators
■ access to informal networks
■ access to information as a resource
■ flexibility in operations.

Viable short-list of marketing opportunity

By matching macro factors in the market with company strengths we can begin to assess the viability of the marketing opportunity. We can classify markets as Hot, Warm or Cold. We target hot prospects first and seek to generate appropriate strategies for warm and cold markets, which may provide opportunities in the future or at a specific lower level of involvement. We can treat cold markets as 'passing trade' and take orders as they may arise, but on our own terms. There is no proactive marketing and no long-term investment in market development in this area. This is covered in more detail in Chapter 3.

Second level decisions

The market

We have already covered macro factors in the level one analysis. The business environment should be known to us at a broad level. We must now consider in detail the viability of the market in which we will compete. We must understand the dynamics and structure of the market. This information is the raw material of the decision-making process and is essential for marketing planning. It is not a luxury. Data gathering at this critical level is often expensive, but the cost should be set against the risk of failure, which is greatly increased without it. What we are trying to establish is the likely level of return on our investment in this market over the time span indicated by corporate objectives.

Taking a product category as an example, we need to know the following information.

▓ What is the extent of local production, ie the total number of units manufactured in the chosen country?
▓ What is the volume of exports from the market?
▓ What is the corresponding volume of imports to the market?

Production less exports plus imports will give you a reasonable idea of what is left in the country to consume. This is called the 'apparent consumption' method of estimating market demand. Obviously this is more appropriate for FMCG products with a fast turnover. For reference information, customs data is generally available free of charge.

To continue the planning process in more depth the firm needs to assess:

▓ market size
▓ volume
▓ value: manufacturer's price, retail price
▓ channel structures
▓ intermediary margins
▓ market structure
▓ volume and value of segments
▓ forecast growth across segments

- regional variations
- competitive structure
- market shares by sector: volume and value
- why has the competition succeeded?
- is this advantage sustainable?
- how might competitors respond? Never assume they will respond in the same way as domestic competition.

The company

We have already considered the basis upon which the company might internationalize its activity. We now need to consider in detail the strengths of the company against the markets targeted. Questions to be asked include.

- Do we know and understand our future customers' needs?
- Do we have experience of this market or similar markets?
- Is the management familiar with local business practices?
- Do we need to develop language skills?
- Can we recruit locally?
- What laws affect local activity (of all kinds)?
- Can we adapt the marketing mix?
- Do we have access to sales support/service in the market?
- Can we sustain this post-sales activity?
- Can we develop and sustain information systems to support local activity?

Level of involvement

The extent to which the above questions can be answered will determine the next stages of the planning process. We are focusing resources and rejecting alternatives as we proceed.

The complexity of international marketing and the different approaches available to the firm are reflected in the planning process. International marketing may be carried out, for example, on the basis of an exploratory marketing approach, fully-fledged exporting and/or even deeper involvement. A different focus will be needed within the plan at each level.

PLANNING FOCUS AT DIFFERENT LEVELS OF INVOLVEMENT

Pre exporting/exploratory:

- Support available
- External facilitators
- Resource availability
- Financing
- Macro business environment
- Information on intermediaries
- Document handling
- Sales effort required
- Communication with customers/intermediaries

Experienced exporters:

- Tracking market trends
- Consumer information
- Product adaptation
- Local communications
- Profit maximization through channel management
- Micro factors in the business environment

The strategic level of involvement in a market will differ as companies enter the international arena. The level of involvement selected will be defined by answering the following questions.

- Will it be sufficient to ensure customer satisfaction?
- Will it be appropriate to the needs and resources of the company?
- Will it match resources with opportunities?
- Will it be sufficient to enter the market successfully?
- Is the level of risk at a manageable level?
- Is it consistent with the organization's objectives?
- What degree of flexibility is required?

Entry method
There is a full range of entry methods to meet the need of the organization and its customers. These range from exporting indirectly through to direct investment in overseas operations. These are discussed further in Chapter 5 and 6. What drives the choice is the match between the organization's objectives and resources, customer needs and the macro/micro environment within which this relationship takes place. If we have carried out the planning

process correctly at this stage we should be able to evaluate alternatives based on full appreciation of these key variables.

Level three decisions

The local marketing plan
This is the plan for the selected overseas market. The local planning process is in principle no different from that in the home market.

▦ Primarily it reflects and is driven by the needs of the local customers.
▦ It establishes a point of difference from the competition in the customers' minds.
▦ It segments the market and targets profitable sectors.
▦ It provides measured objectives against which progress can be measured.
▦ It reflects the context in which the relationship between the company and its customers takes place.
▦ It provides the basis for future activity based on market information and research.

Other functional areas of the plan
In international markets we must consider the implications of marketing plans on the other areas of the business. International marketing will be driven by the marketing function within an organization, but 'international', as we have said, reconfigures the whole organization. Marketing is responsible for creating and managing customer relationships, and therefore is the key driver of profitable business. The marketing function will lead the way overseas, but other functions must be assessed in terms of their capability to deliver.

Operations
We must consider the following questions.

▦ Production planning – can we handle increased orders and reschedule production timetables?
▦ Can we handle product adaptation?
▦ Can we source raw materials?
▦ Are there particular packaging laws or requirements for recycling the product packaging?

■ Can we manage increased inventory?
■ Can we cope with overseas logistics and distribution?
■ Do we understand export documentation procedures?
■ Are information technology support systems transferable?
■ Can we network with intermediaries overseas?

Finance

■ Can we be sure of getting paid?
■ Can we handle foreign currency transactions?
■ Can we manage cash flows and deal with time lag in payment?
■ Can we increase our working capital?
■ Can we handle alternative payment such as countertrade?
■ Are we confident that there is no political threat to overseas investment?
■ Can we cost the venture?
■ What is the real profit available?

People: getting organized for the new venture

■ Are they experienced international marketers?
■ Can they adapt to change?
■ What is their skills base?
■ Do they understand overseas business practice?
■ Can we retain existing staff?
■ Can we recruit to fill skills gaps?

Level four decisions

Coordinating the international plan

At this stage of the plan we resite the local plan into the main framework of business planning for our organization. We will almost certainly be limited in the number of markets we can enter. Decisions have to be made about which markets receive priority and funding. We must consider the impact on our home markets. We must be careful not to take our eye off our key markets (customers) in order to concentrate on the new market opportunities.

This problem can be approached in several ways. First, we can set up an international division, which has a degree of autonomy, and raises finance 'independently' of the home operation. Or we can bed the overseas operations within existing activity and ensure that they are controlled through the process of coordinating the various international marketing plans centrally. Ultimately the aim is to maximize profits for the organization as a whole. The complexities of portfolio management should not concern the new exporter, but they become an issue when overseas operations expand.

The international organization
The company must have in place a clear organizational framework which enables the current and future situations to be controlled as the level of internationalization increases. This may mean that central control is devolved to local operations or alternatively that further centralization takes place. Solutions must be appropriate to the needs and objectives of the business and balanced against the level of risk in the international environment to which the business is exposed. Above all, the organization must be configured in such a way that it can listen and react to customers' changing needs.

In the recent past this has generally meant that major multinationals are decentralizing, and are pushing power down to operational levels where middle managers have greater awareness of customers' requirements.

When we evaluate structures we need to consider the following.

■ Responsibilities must be clearly allocated.
■ Reporting lines must be well defined.
■ Managers must communicate.
■ The various local subsidiaries must be encouraged to share good practice.
■ IT must be embedded in the organization's structures.
■ Objectives should be established through negotiation.
■ All business functions must be involved.
■ The local 'voice' must be respected.
■ Suppliers and consumers must be incorporated into the decision-making process.
■ Negotiation, collaboration and consultation must be included as a participating process.
■ Flexibility in implementation must be capable of being accommodated to allow for change.

The corporate plan
This frequently embraces the paradoxical statement that what is required is a balance between the corporate need for conformity, standardized information and accountability expressed through standard reporting procedures, set against the need to get closer to

customers through diversity of operations and decentralization. This perfect balance is rarely achieved. Reporting is important, but it should not be so prescriptive that it stifles local innovation and creativity where the customers, together with the nature and basis of the market-place, demand it.

The corporate planning process must take full account of local market requirements. Success, profitability and share price are ultimately functions of success in marketing products and satisfying customers over time.

SUMMARY

Planning is the process of matching the resources of the organization with opportunities in the market-place. In the often seemingly chaotic environment that exists in international markets the planning process attempts to impose a degree of order.

Business must recognize the key differences in planning for international marketing. There is no off-the-shelf planning solution. Packaged solutions simply do not work. Even the most sophisticated organizations recognize and accept this. We propose a framework that can be adopted by organizations wishing to internationalize their activity or extend existing international marketing effort. The framework identifies four levels of decision making.

Level one concerns the decision to internationalize. Internationalization must start at the top of an organization and be embraced by the corporate mission. We scan the international environment for opportunities, assessing the macro environment against the company's competencies and ability to manage the international business. As a result of this process we are left with a short-list of potential markets ranked in order of the organization's ability to exploit identified opportunities.

Level two: as we narrow the scanning process we seek to affect a market–company match. We analyse the market dynamics, including customers and competitive behaviour, against company objectives and capabilities. The result is a decision as to the appropriate strategic level of involvement, which will dictate the preferred market entry strategy, from indirect exporting through to direct investment.

At Level three the local marketing plan is developed, which will include the effect on other functional areas of the business and the organization that will support international activity. This will cover local objectives, segmentation, targeting and positioning, and as such will direct the configuration of the mix and the development of a tactical plan with controls, contingencies and budgets.

Level four completes the planning cycle and feeds local marketing activity into the international business plan and, in turn, into the corporate plan. The company must create an international culture and the method of managing this is at least as important as the structures within which management takes place. We must achieve a balance between control and creativity appropriate to the market and customer requirements.

5

Managing the Strategic Level of Involvement – Exporting Directly and Indirectly

INTRODUCTION

Correct evaluation, selection and management of entry strategies are vital for success. Strategic decisions at this level represent the key link between an organization and its customers. Intermediaries, for example are, in the eyes of customers, the organization. Careful management of the process is imperative.

In an age in which real innovation is difficult, it has been said that channel management and the management of brand equity are the keys to success in the current marketing environment. The process of expanding the business internationally exposes the organization to risk in both these key business areas. It must be managed correctly.

We have discussed the process of planning for international marketing. We have been through the process of evaluating information. We have established the desired level of involvement and indicated potential entry strategies to achieve this goal.

The key benefit of planning was to match resources and opportunities. However, in international marketing we are also attempting to minimize the risk to which we will be exposed. Risk is an inevitable part of business activity, but through careful planning and the adoption of an appropriate strategy it can be minimized – or if not minimized, planned for.

International marketing is about the relationship between an organization and its overseas customers. Entry strategies provide the essential link between the parties in this relationship. It is clear that the entry decision has far-reaching strategic implications. Essentially it revolves around the question 'How close do I need to be to my customer in order to succeed?'. Entry strategies are an important part of the strategic armoury. They are obviously offensive marketing weapons, but they involve greater or lesser degrees of risk and provide the marketer with a greater or lesser degree of control over this risk.

THE INTERNATIONAL MARKETING BATTLEFIELD – DRAWING UP THE BATTLE LINES

The choice of entry strategy:

■ sets out the rules and scope of the terms of engagement with the competition
■ confirms the extent and the seriousness of commitment to the local market
■ determines the parameters in planning for and managing the local market
■ precludes certain tactical activity and determines the nature of long-term strategy
■ once committed to is often hard to change without substantial risk and often incurs financial penalties
■ is therefore always associated with an equally well-considered exit strategy.

It is the ability of the international marketer to configure the need for profit with exposure to risk through strategic control that will determine success or failure. As can be seen in Figure 5.1, there is a range of strategies available, and companies depending on their exposure in the international arena may be dealing with different levels of strategic involvement in different markets. For example, if a company was approaching Russia as a market, the degree of risk

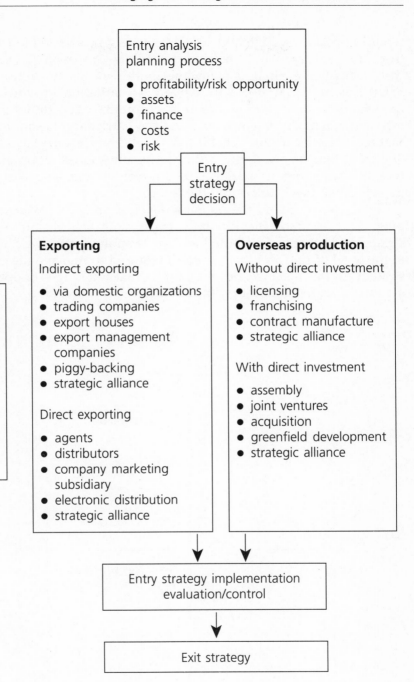

Figure 5.1 *Entry strategy alternatives (Lewis and Housden, 1998)*

would be relatively high and strategies would be selected to reflect this. The converse would be true in selecting Australia. Countries can be further evaluated using the model shown in Figure 5.2. What this model attempts to explain is a situation in which the organization has identified a high-level country opportunity in the international marketing area, and analysis carried out has indicated that its strengths are such that it has a high-level resource available to exploit the perceived opportunity. This unusual situation means that the entire range of market entry strategies is available to exploit the opportunities ie to occupy the 'space'.

The circles represent the potential level of profitability available over the period of the planning cycle from the various entry strategies. These are distributed within the strategic space according to the level of risk and the resources required to manage the entry strategy. In this instance, despite the fact that full ranges of options are available, the greatest profit is available from licensing.

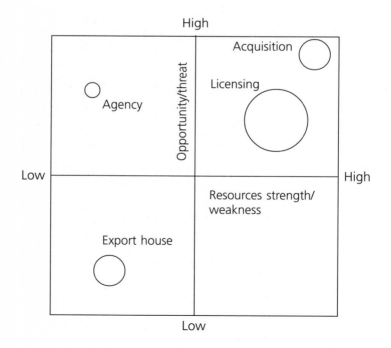

Figure 5.2 *International strategic space map – 1*

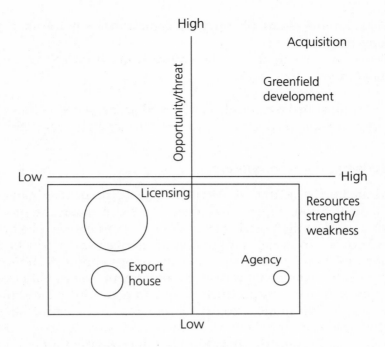

Figure 5.3 *International strategic space map – 2*

In Figure 5.3 the research carried out by the company indicates a weaker opportunity, and the resources available to exploit this opportunity are equally reduced. This excludes certain strategic options, as they are unprofitable, but indicates that at lower levels certain risk options may be profitable. In this case, licensing is again the most attractive option. Thus we can see that it is possible that a market entry strategy can apply in more than one set of circumstances.

ENTRY ANALYSIS

Before determining the precise details of market entry, the firm must focus on the answers to the following questions.

▥ What level of profit is available in the chosen market?
▥ Over what time-scale?
▥ What assets do we require? We must look at capital, labour, machinery and human resource requirements.

- What are the affordable financial commitments in the short and long term?
- What costs, both direct and indirect, are involved in implementation?

The firm must make carefully considered judgements on these key factors and relate its decision to the options available for entry.

Consideration of the options

There are two broad options. We can make the product at home and transport it to our target market(s), or we can make the product overseas in the target market or a country of our choice. The first is described as exporting and the second as overseas production or foreign direct investment. The range of options appear in Figure 5.1.

There is no sequential process or requirement to start with export and move to overseas production and foreign direct investment. Clearly, for the smaller company the resources available will preclude some options. However, a small company can gain a global presence quite quickly through the development of strategic alliances, licensing or franchise agreements, or even electronic distribution of, say, information-based products.

In today's virtual reality market-place, smaller companies have access to global markets through a wide variety of channels – an option previously available only to major corporations. The global imperative is therefore as much a concern for small companies as it is for the larger players.

We do not intend to go into detail about the processes involved in setting up a strategic alliance, joint venture or franchise. Each case will need to be considered on its own merits and experts will need to be consulted to ensure that legal requirements are followed and that contracts are valid. However, we can point to some of the pitfalls that exist, and of course these must be considered when evaluating entry methods.

Indirect exporting

We begin at the lowest level of strategic involvement, control and risk, and move along the continuum of deepening involvement.

Option 1: domestic purchasing

Definition
Product sold to overseas companies represented in the home market and bought by them in the home market. In effect, the exporter is treating the overseas opportunity exactly as if it were a domestic one.

Matrix position (Figure 5.2)

■ low perceived market opportunity
■ potentially high-risk environment
■ low resource/international skills level required
■ inexperienced international marketing.

When to use this strategy
This is a useful way to start international activity. It is the lowest level of involvement, but introduces the company to the needs of overseas customers. This may be a toehold in international markets, which can lead to deepening involvement and profitable relationships.

Things to watch out for
Low margin activity and low control over where the product goes and what price it is sold at.

■ Companies wishing to develop internationally must move beyond this stage very quickly. There is a fundamental lack of knowledge about the market and the end user.
■ The company relies on the whim of the purchaser. Lose this customer and your international ambitions are over for now.
■ It is difficult to understand and sustain an advantage internationally (eg why do international companies/customers buy the product?). There is little or at best low-level international learning curve activity.

Making it work

■ Get close to the purchasing company.
■ Look for ongoing supply contracts.
■ Research the buyer's end user market.
■ Look for similar deals elsewhere.

◼ Don't be reactive.
◼ Be proactive. Search out locally based buyers.
◼ Learn whatever you can – fast – and be prepared to move on.

Examples

Department store buyers from the major stores in Japan and the USA buy from UK suppliers. Many multinational organizations will have a 'procurement office' sourcing from domestic (UK) suppliers.

Option 2: international trading companies

Definition

International conglomerates with wide-ranging activities in many markets. Often based on colonial trading companies, but now with a substantial diversified portfolio, from cement to cars to cocoa; eg Lonrho or Inchcape.

When is it appropriate?

The size and geographic coverage of these substantial organizations make them attractive international partners. They usually have excellent credit ratings.

Matrix position (Figure 5.2)

◼ potentially high risk
◼ low skills base
◼ low opportunity.

Things to watch out for

◼ Negative association with images of imperialism (eg colonial heritage).
◼ Lower margins – the trading partner is doing the work and will justifiably want rewarding.
◼ Control over marketing – there may be very little.
◼ Commoditization of your product – lack of marketing invites commoditization.
◼ Sporadic order-taking.
◼ Lack of long-term commitment.
◼ *Ad hoc* nature makes planning for long-term involvement difficult.

Making it work

■ Go for long-term supply contracts.
■ Seek partners with complementary geographic activity.
■ Extend from your base.
■ Research end user market.

Further examples
East Asiatic Corporation, Jardine Mathieson, Sime Derby, United Africa Company, C-Itoh, Mitsubishi.

Option 3: export houses

Definition
This category includes:

■ export merchants: these simply buy the company's products and sell them abroad
■ confirming houses: these take ownership of the company's products and provide access to higher risk markets
■ manufacturers' home-based export agents: these are based in the home market and handle exports for a company with payment based on commission. (Export agents do not take ownership of the product.)

When is it appropriate?

■ when payment is difficult
■ when there is a high degree of risk attached
■ when the company cannot manage the export overhead
■ when there are short-term problems in the home market
■ to kick start further international involvement
■ particularly suitable for small to medium-sized enterprises (SME). Around 60 per cent of SMEs involved in exporting use export houses of one kind.

Matrix position (Figure 5.2)

■ higher risk markets, particularly those with currency problems
■ inexperienced in international marketing
■ lower opportunities.

Things to watch out for

■ Control is extremely limited, especially in the choice of the product–market match and marketing support (ie the firm may not be involved in the selection of the market(s) that its products go to).
■ Short-term approach; there is no real relationship-building with market intermediaries or the end user.
■ This entry option is not fully linked to strategy; it is hard to bring this mode into the corporate framework.
■ This is a limited international strategy. It is simply an extension of the domestic marketing strategy.
■ There is little learning about overseas marketing.
■ It is unfocused.

Making it work

■ Choose partners carefully.
■ Use the experience of trade associations and local Chambers of Commerce for guidance.
■ Monitor the contract carefully.
■ Research the end user market if possible.

Examples
There are 800 export houses in the UK. Their activities usually focus on market sectors or countries. The Institute of Export is a useful source of information.

Option 4: export management companies

Definition
These are similar to export houses, but the export management company (EMC) will constitute a virtual export department for the company. It will provide all the functions of an in-house export department without the cost implications.

When is it appropriate?

■ when the organization has a firm strategic approach to exporting
■ when the company wishes to learn and build on initial exposure to international markets
■ when it is felt important to have a deeper understanding of the market and a higher degree of control in the market

■ when the nature of the product is such that it requires a higher degree of involvement locally (for example service requirements).
■ when the company cannot take on the full financial risk of international marketing.

Matrix position (Figure 5.2)

■ inexperienced.
■ Levels of risk are countered by a higher degree of opportunity.

Things to watch out for

■ The relationship must be equal and sustainable.
■ Contracts must be carefully drawn up.
■ Beware of outsourcing the development of critical expertise.
■ If the EMC succeeds, it is in danger of doing itself out of a good job. This relationship needs to be managed on both sides.
■ Look out for EMCs with market expertise as well as product knowledge. Technical skills are no substitute for insight and knowledge of an overseas market.
■ Different EMCs may be required for different regional or national markets.
■ This method of entry is suitable for SMEs and for larger companies looking at small markets.

Making it work

■ Take legal advice.
■ Work with individuals you can get on with.
■ Focus on sustaining the relationship.
■ Build the relationship through limited exposure across product lines.
■ Manage across all EMCs. Get them to talk to each other. Organize a conference and invite them to participate.
■ Plan for success in partnership. Plan how much business will be generated and set mutually acceptable objectives over the life of the collaboration.
■ Decide what profit you will take.

Examples
There are a range of companies that can help in this area. Export consultants registered with the Chartered Institute of Marketing (CIM) may also help.

Option 5: piggy-backing

Definition

A lot is talked about piggy-backing but very little is done in this area. Larger companies do use piggy-backing, and for some it is important, but essentially it is not a popular route to overseas markets for UK companies.

Piggy-backing is an agreement between two companies, one with established international marketing activity and the other with a complementary product range which is not marketed in certain countries. The company with the established channels and know-how is used to market the products of the other. Complementarity is defined around the market or routes to market rather than production or supply. In this sense there is an element that resembles a strategic alliance.

When is it appropriate?

■ when there is a perceived opportunity in the target market but a low level of experience or expertise in the rider company
■ where a combination of products will complement and enhance the presence of both companies in the target market
■ when a low level of financial investment is required
■ when existing distributor channels are not present or under-developed (eg China)
■ when the benefits of the carrier's image are transferred to the rider
■ when there is a tight link with the carrier and a focus on market needs.

Matrix position (Figure 5.2)

■ Low experience in particular markets.
■ The risk for the carrier is high due to the low involvement of the rider company.

Things to watch out for

■ Method of payment: by commission or does the carrier take ownership?
■ Which brand takes the lead in the local market: that of the carrier or the rider?

- The carrier holds the cards as the lead partner. The customer interfaces with the end user.
- The rider is vulnerable to product development by the carrier or even acquisition.
- Branding and promotional strategies need to be developed carefully. The portrayal of two brands may create confusion.

Making it work

- Partner choice is critically important.
- Keep the arrangement flexible.
- Develop a trusting and open relationship.
- Focus on the market. Look for a configuration that will add value in the eyes of the customer from the synergy created by the 'superior' offering.

Examples
Minolta and IBM in the USA; Olivetti and AT&T in Europe and the USA; Colgate Palmolive and Wilkinson Sword.

Direct exporting

Introduction
Indirect exporting is a low-risk strategy which often approaches the international market as an extension of the domestic operation. As has been said, committed international marketing is far more complex than this. It involves a strategic, long-term view of the identification, anticipation and satisfaction of customer needs. As we develop this strategic approach, it is clear that the levels of risk to which the organization is exposed might increase.

Profitability may be compromised as a result of a more committed approach to international marketing, at least in the short term; hence the real need for planning and all that that entails. Entry strategies are selected against levels of opportunity. It may be that risk is so high as to preclude anything other than indirect exporting. This is most unusual, however, and the option of direct exporting will reflect the strategic planning which informs a deeper level of involvement.

Although there may be a short-term improvement in profitability available through indirect international marketing this is almost certainly not sustainable as we are remote from our customers.

The key consideration is whether profitability increases despite greater involvement. Greater investment usually means a larger exposure to risk.

Another important factor revolves around the organization's ability to handle the gearing up of all activity through the entire organization. This is necessary as the level of involvement increases.

At this stage of involvement all the business functions become involved in international marketing. This is the first stage in the independent management of the international process. The organization must be prepared for the challenges this will produce. Figure 5.4 presents in diagrammatic form the possible relationship between profit and investment as the organization crosses the threshold from indirect to direct involvement in international market entry strategy.

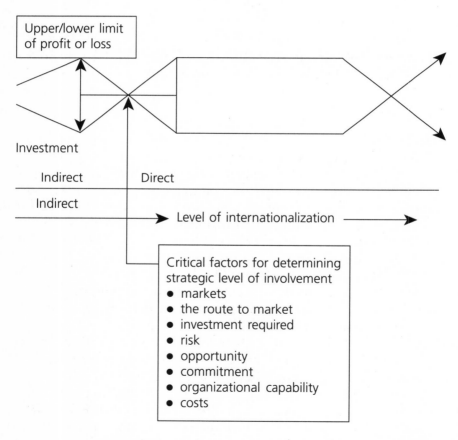

Figure 5.4 *The relationship between profit and investment, depending on international market entry strategy*

Option 6: agents and distributors

Definition

Agents act as intermediaries between the company and its customers. Agents never take ownership of the product or service but take a commission on contract between the customer and the principal (the company). Specialists in the field of international marketing will point to situations where agents do collect money for the principal. However, in the process of describing increasing international involvement and differentiating between agents and distributors this definition is both sufficient and technically correct.

Distributors differ from agents in that they take title to the product and sell on their own account. Effectively the distributor becomes the customer. The distributor takes the risk, whereas agents take no risk. It is generally a higher involvement strategy. Additionally, there is more involvement for the manufacturer in the marketing and support of the product. Distributors will generally be closer to the manufacturer and will allow greater knowledge to be gained about the overseas market.

When is it appropriate?

■ when there is a low level of overseas experience in the manu-facturing firm
■ when there is a perceived level of risk in the target market
■ generally agents are appropriate for high-value products; distrib-utors are appropriate for wide-distribution high-volume products
■ when the relationship between supplier and end user is complex and knowledge of the cultural imperatives is required in the transaction
■ when there are significant barriers to entry for the manufacturing firm
■ when local distribution is complex a distributor may be appro-priate
■ when the agent has substantial experience in the marketing of products in local markets
■ when there are barriers to repatriation of profit.

Matrix position (Figure 5.2)

■ reasonable opportunity
■ high risk

■ low control
■ low experience.

Things to watch out for

■ agents handling competing products
■ inexperience in marketing
■ loss of control of brand identity
■ ability to terminate the contract may be difficult
■ financial/credit rating of the agent/distributor
■ relationship with local influencers and institutions
■ infrastructure, logistical capacity, IT and after-sales service which may have to be 'delivered' by the domestic manufacturer.

Making it work

■ Contracts must be drawn up with care. Take legal advice; EU law now favours the agent/distributor above the principal.
■ Build the relationship; look to manage the contract. Collaboration should be key.
■ The principal must be clear on what the important issues are.
■ Great care must be taken in selecting, appointing, managing and motivating the 'partnership'.
■ The extent of activity across markets and product areas is another crucial consideration to avoid confusion and parallel import activity.
■ The financial commitment of both parties must be determined. Discount structures must be clearly defined and the manner and time of payment must be specified.
■ Which country's law will prevail in case of dispute and arbitration must be decided in advance.
■ The duration of the agreement and termination procedures must be established.

Examples

The DTI publishes information on managing agents and distributors. It also provides an evaluation service for locating appropriate agents/distributors.

Lekkerland acts as a distributor in the confectionery industry in Europe acting for several companies and covering a highly fragmented retail market.

Option 7: company marketing subsidiary

Definition
This involves setting up a local operation to work within the overseas market via a locally recruited sales force or expatriate staff. This market entry option can cover all activity with the exception of manufacturing, and will usually cover importing, marketing and possibly distribution locally. This is a major fundamental step forward in the level of involvement. It is the first step into a foreign market involving the organization's direct commitment to money, people and logistics. The costs escalate dramatically, and this step should only be undertaken if the firm has achieved a high degree of learning, insight and understanding of the market and its culture, business etiquette, laws, etc. This level of risk has jumped to a high magnitude. This is the first real step into the 'unknown'.

The subsidiary will reflect the character of the parent organization and may be a substantial operation or a small one-person office.

When is it appropriate?

▧ when there are tax advantages to direct operation
▧ when there is a complex after-sales requirement
▧ high level of opportunity compared with risk
▧ when market entry is part of a long-term commitment to the international market
▧ when there is complex behaviour in the end user market
▧ when a higher level of control is required, particularly over marketing
▧ when business practice or local regulation demands a physical presence
▧ when an organization is working in a regional market using a marketing subsidiary as a hub for regional development using alternative entry strategies.

Matrix position (Figure 5.2)

▧ high opportunity compared with risk
▧ high control
▧ long-term opportunity

Things to watch out for

- ■ local regulation on employment
- ■ potential expropriation of assets
- ■ issues of taxation
- ■ differences between local business practice/etiquette and the domestic experience
- ■ understanding the local market dynamics
- ■ local reaction to expatriate managers
- ■ higher start-up costs
- ■ time to start-up is extended
- ■ difficulty in recruiting suitably experienced individuals.

This is a high-involvement strategy; there is substantial risk in a long-term strategy of increasing involvement if this is not carried through successfully. Failure may mean that it is very hard to re-establish a presence in the market.

Making it work

- ■ Commitment of resources evaluated against opportunity.
- ■ This strategy is more suited to a liberal/deregulated business environment.
- ■ Establish cultural 'closeness'.
- ■ Expand IT capability for control.
- ■ Learn from the market.
- ■ Enhance home administration to cope with the additional demands.

SUMMARY

The decision on entry strategy is critical and is a strategic decision. It involves the balancing of risk and opportunity, with the key factor being the level of return required on the investment in international marketing. The key to this is the requirement to identify, anticipate and satisfy customer needs over time. Entry strategies will determine the organization's ability to do this.

In this chapter we presented a flow chart for the assessment of entry strategies and a number of planning matrices which help to make the connections between risk opportunity and levels of return.

The strategic space map is a useful vehicle for the assessment of entry methods.

The chapter moved on to consider the indirect and direct methods of exporting, and suggested when the various options are appropriate, potential problems in the management of this risk and how best to make these strategies work.

6

Managing the Strategic Level of Involvement in Production Overseas

INTRODUCTION

Starting to produce overseas raises the strategic level of involvement to new heights. It is at this juncture the company becomes seriously committed to international activity in the long term and in doing so it becomes exposed to higher levels of risk.

The motives for overseas manufacture vary substantially. A key variable to consider is that the firm may well not be producing in the country for which the product is manufactured.

In producing overseas the company may be taking advantage of any of the following:

- cheap labour
- access to raw materials
- proximity to key subcontractors
- tax avoidance
- capitalising on host government incentives
- gaining the advantage of being perceived as a 'local' company.
- the country of manufacture is part of a regional trading bloc.

The key consideration is that from the country of manufacture we have access to markets for our products or services. This does not demand geographical proximity.

In today's international arena plastic bags for the British retail trade are now manufactured in China. Nike training shoes are subcontracted to manufacturers in the sout-east Asian market. Ford engines are made in Brazil. What companies do as 'manufacturers' is to configure the production process in such a way as to enable them to deliver maximum benefit to their customers in whatever way they require it and in doing so maintaining a sustainable level of advantage over their competition. This may require taking control of the process directly, or it may involve licensing, franchising, subcontracting, joint ventures or strategic alliances.

The choice depends on the nature of the business we are in, the customers being served and what values they seek, set against the level of risk, the level of opportunity and the potential returns to the organization over time.

The example was given earlier of how the Ford Galaxy, the Volkswagen Sharon and the Seat Alhambra are produced via a joint venture in Portugal called AutoEuropa. The companies differentiate on other factors, such as branding and levels of service. They compete against each other and other producers on price. The joint venture in production lowered the cost of production, which in turn means that all three companies can compete in the highly competitive European MPV sector. How far the partners in production compete against each other on price is determined by the value they can extract individually from the rest of the process of delivering satisfaction to customers (the brand, etc.).

PRODUCTION WITHOUT DIRECT INVESTMENT

Option 1: licensing

Definition
Confers the right to utilize a company-specific patent, trademark, copyright or process for an agreed fee, in a given country, over a prescribed time span.

When is it appropriate?

■ when companies wish to avoid the risk of product or market development by exploiting the expertise of the licenser and licensee in product development and marketing
■ when there is a political risk of expropriation, this is reduced through the relationship with a local operator
■ when it reduces the exposure to risk and to financial commitment in fixed assets
■ when there is a need for regular cash returns. Fees should be guaranteed and regular
■ when there are high costs of transportation
■ when rapid penetration of many markets is required
■ when there are significant tariff or non-tariff barriers to entry.

Licensing provides a useful entry method to international markets for SMEs who might otherwise lack the resources or expertise to develop at the pace required to maximize return.

Matrix position (Figure 5.2)

■ higher risk compared with opportunity
■ low control.

Things to watch out for

■ The licenser runs the risk of creating a competitor at the end of the term of the agreement. This may even extend to home markets.
■ It is hard to police territorial arrangements.
■ Returns are generally low, if regular. The licensee will seek the major reward; average returns may be as low as 5 per cent of gross sales, but vary from 2–3 per cent for industrial products to maybe 30 per cent for products with a shorter life cycle.
■ There must be an attractive offer to overseas licensees. The licenser must licence an advantage. A 'me too' product will be unlikely to succeed.
■ Control of quality will be difficult and may compromise longer term viability in the targeted market.
■ Long-term market development on the part of the licenser may be difficult.
■ Renewal of a successful contract will almost certainly require a commitment to innovation on the part of the licenser.

- The licensee will be free to choose technology, etc., that will best deliver benefits to its customers.
- There may be problems of communicating complex technologies across cultures.
- Negotiation may be complex in that little real information will be given away by the licenser due to the risks associated with the failure of negotiation.
- Problems over the timing and nature of fees.

Making it work

- Select the licensee carefully.
- Contracts need to be carefully drawn up and only entered into after taking specialist legal advice.
- Identify clearly the benefits the licensee will receive.
- Ensure that rights are clearly identifiable and easily transferable.
- Actively manage the contract.
- Seek equity in the licensee; bring the companies closer together.
- Set geographic limits that fit with the international strategy of the company.
- Ensure the competence of the licensee, not just in terms of technology but also in terms of the ability to market the product and support after-sales activity.
- It is advisable that the licenser retains control over key components.
- Register everything possible in the name of the licenser.
- Use patent and trade mark protection to help manage the process.

Examples

Coca-Cola licenses local production but supplies the cola essence itself. The licensees add 99 per cent local ingredients – water! Cadbury licenses the rights to its brands in the USA to Hershey. In the brewing sector there are many examples. Heineken, the Dutch lager, is brewed under licence in the UK by Whitbread.

Option 2: franchising

Definition

This option has similarities to licensing but generally involves greater management commitment. Franchising involves the full process of overseas operations from production through to marketing and after-sales service.

Jain defines franchising as 'when a company grants an individual or business the right or privilege to do business for a consideration from the franchisee in a prescribed manner over a certain period of time in a prescribed place'.

When is it appropriate?

■ when there is a high degree of peripheral activity around the core product
■ when the business is intensively focused on service or people
■ when the target market has a suitable human resource infrastructure but capital may be scarce
■ when there is a requirement to enter a number of overseas markets at speed
■ when a substantial degree of control is required over all elements of the marketing mix
■ when there are limited resources in the parent company to develop a product or service
■ when the local political situation dictates a high level of local involvement
■ when local culture demands it.

Matrix position (Figure 5.2)

■ high control compared with risk
■ good opportunity.

Things to watch out for

■ Cultural differences in service standards may cause problems.
■ The extent to which the entire management processes can be adopted by the franchisee.
■ Cultural and environmental factors that may demand or benefit from adaptation.
■ Optimization of the market – product match may not occur in this case.
■ Lack of either market information or market focus. Franchising may be based on an attractive way of doing business rather than on an attractive marketing opportunity. Beware of this danger.
■ Franchisee must have the skills base to manage the entire operation as specified by the franchisor; this must be carefully assessed and balanced against market expectations.

▪ Quality assurance is vital.
▪ The franchisor management team must be multidisciplined and multiskilled.

Making it work

▪ Franchising must be selected on the basis of sound international marketing planning.
▪ The appropriateness of the franchise package to the overseas market must be assessed carefully.
▪ The franchisee should be treated in the first instance as an intermediary between the company and the market (customer).
▪ The degree of adaptability of the elements of the package must be agreed in advance and the responsibilities allocated between the parties.
▪ The agreement must have a rigorous legal base, including a time frame.

Examples

Examples of successful franchise operations on an international basis include Benetton, Pizza Hut, 7-Eleven, McDonald's and Body Shop.

Option 3: contract manufacture

Definition

A third party produces goods under contract. All other activity is the responsibility of the contractor. In the past this has related to the process of physical production of goods. Today the concept can be extended to include any component of the process of delivery of the offer to customers. For example, BA's ticketing operation is handled in Mumbai (Bombay) and its catering is handled by contract caterers in their local markets. This process of analysis of the value chain is a vital area in sustaining advantage and is one that all businesses must examine. Advantages in price, quality or service offer may be gained through outsourcing under 'contract'.

In addition companies can opt for an assembly type operation in overseas markets, supplying components which are put together and finished in an overseas market. This option is variously described as CKD (completely knocked down) production or screwdriver plants.

When is it appropriate?

- when there is a demand for a degree of local content
- when local manufacture is cheaper – wage rates particularly
- when local raw materials are available and at lower cost
- when particular process skills are more advanced
- when political risk is high, thus avoiding the potential expropriation of assets
- when a rapid exit strategy may be required due to political problems
- when high control of the marketing process is required
- when there is oversupply in local manufacturing capacity and producers can be 'played off' against each other
- when there is a small local market which will not justify investment in plant
- when capital can be better employed in other areas of the business
- when links to third markets are better established from the producing country
- if a long-term acquisition strategy is possible.

Matrix position (Figure 5.2)

- high risk compared with opportunity
- high control.

Things to watch out for

- Quality control requires careful monitoring, constantly.
- The degree of unionization/state of labour relations in the manufacturing company is a further important consideration.
- Threat of acquisition by competitor.
- Stability of partner organization.
- Length of contract, be it a 'one-off' or longer term.
- Does quality simply relate to the product or are environmental issues a factor? Will production methods impact on the firm's corporate or marketing image (for example the use or abuse of child labour, polluting factories, etc.).

Making it work

- A full audit of the partner is required in terms of all its activities and how they will impact on the end user market.

- It is important to form a relationship with the manufacturer.
- Specify all conditions within the contract. Price may not be the key driver in the target market.
- Ensure alternative suppliers are available.
- Spread the risk if necessary.
- Scan for global opportunities. The costs of logistics and distribution are falling dramatically, and this makes international contract manufacture a rapidly expanding area of activity.

Examples
S R Gent in Sri Lanka produces clothing for Marks & Spencer and many other UK clothing retailers. Seventy per cent of the world's hand-stitched footballs are made in Pakistan.

PRODUCTION WITH DIRECT INVESTMENT

Introduction

The process of investment in fixed assets in overseas markets takes the organization further into deepening involvement in international marketing.

The process of market evaluation and selection must be rigorously adhered to. The company must understand all aspects of the market and local business practice before making the decision. The levels of risk must be set against the organization's ability to deal with failure. Remember that failure may not be solely associated with withdrawal from the market, but may include underperforming against investment. There are many companies which have been acquired as a result of unfulfilled ambition in the international market-place. Shares in the home market are consequently devalued and they become targets for takeover. Mistakes will almost certainly be expensive. Shareholders must be supportive of the strategic decision, as it will almost certainly affect dividend levels in the short term, although the decision is clearly made with a view to increased returns over time.

Issues against:

- Costly in resources.
- Takes management's eye off the home market.
- Demands that the company has the systems capacity to manage all activity.

- Political sensitivity to the potential disruption of local economies, companies and market structures.
- Expropriation is always a factor to consider.
- There is no cultural bridge through the use of intermediaries.
- The repatriation of profits may be problematical.

Ownership has substantial benefits however.

- 100 per cent ownership = 100 per cent of profits.
- It eliminates the ramifications of managing partners.
- It allows total control and enables the organization to learn.
- It adds prestige and value, perhaps beyond the asset value of the investment.
- It gears the organization up at all levels to compete in the global market.
- Ability to benefit from transfer pricing, maximising tax advantages at all levels.
- Freedom of manoeuvring within international operations to avoid legal obligation in any one market.
- Influence over local political decisions.
- Creating 'insiderization' in regional economies, avoiding quotas, etc.
- Taking advantage of local government incentives, tax breaks, etc.
- Economies of scale may be the key to competitiveness.

Whilst direct investment implies a greater level of strategic involvement in markets, there are various lower cost routes to explore before full green field development. These include acquisitions and joint ventures.

Option 1: assembly

Definition
Components of production are shipped and brought together at a wholly owned site. Components may be supplied by other companies or produced by the same company. Shared production is increasingly common in, for example, the automotive sector. These are often referred to as screwdriver sites.

When is it appropriate?

▓ when assembly operations can take place in a free trade zone
▓ when there are high tariffs or quotas on import of the finished product
▓ when the local origin effect is pronounced
▓ when there is a short lifespan for the finished product
▓ when cost control and pricing are key local drivers
▓ when government pressure for local employment is strong
▓ when optimization of capital against labour skills/labour costs is required
▓ when the cost of transporting finished product across borders is higher than the various components
▓ when insiderization is important (eg in regional markets).

Matrix position (Figure 5.2)

▓ good opportunity lowers risk
▓ high control.

Things to watch out for

▓ local employment consideration, degree of unionization, local employment regulations
▓ economic and social stability of the country
▓ potential volatility in trade tariffs or quotas on components
▓ political stability of the local government
▓ strong transportation infrastructure
▓ availability of local management skills and human resources.

Making it work

▓ Ensure that full local support for operations is available.
▓ Invest in recruitment and training.
▓ Commitment is vital at all levels.
▓ Focus on TQM (total quality management).

Examples
Examples are extremely varied, covering most industrial consumer fields – automotive, farming equipment, computer hardware and recently personal computers.

Option 2: joint ventures

Definition
Two companies come together to create a third in which each holds equity, although not necessarily equally. The third company exists as a company in itself and the partners benefit in proportion to the equity stake or in accordance with the joint venture agreement.

When is it appropriate?

■ when there is a legal barrier to independent operation in a country
■ where local input or knowledge is desirable
■ when there is a higher degree of risk
■ if available capital is limited or capital investment is shared but the capital invested is leveraged to its full extent
■ when profit opportunities in a higher risk environment need to be maximized
■ when there is a perceived long-term involvement
■ when R&D costs are high
■ when complementary skills exist pooling resources may achieve better results
■ when access to local capital markets is required
■ when rapid international development is required
■ when a stable regional beachhead is required.

Matrix position (Figure 5.2)

■ higher risk compared with opportunity
■ lower control

Things to watch out for

■ Partner choice is absolutely critical.
■ Potential conflicts of interest between joint venture partners must be recognized and planned for together.
■ Locating the joint venture within the strategic framework of the organizations over time.
■ Beware of an imbalance in activity between the partners leading to the development of a blame culture.
■ Exit strategies may be complex; divorce is expensive!
■ Joint ventures should be used to extend capabilities rather than just extending competitive advantage.

■ Defining complementarity over time may be difficult.
■ Identification of a common strategic goal.

Making it work

■ Clearly define the scope of the business, expectations and objectives.
■ Staff the venture with local employees, or at the very least involve them in the decision-making process at operational levels.
■ Create a company of sufficient size to act as a regional hub.
■ Take expert advice.
■ Base the venture on market- (customer-) based benefits.
■ Balance inputs between parties.
■ Consider the extent of the local influence of potential partners.
■ Determine how profits will be accumulated and distributed; as Terpstra puts it: 'Pay out or Plough Back'.
■ Access to senior managers in both partners is essential.
■ Do not over-control from the centre.
■ Manage information exchange carefully; IT systems must be compatible.
■ Realize that patience is a virtue; set realistic early objectives.
■ Benchmark against similar joint venture operations.

Examples
Cereal Partners is the result of the joint venture between General Mills and Nestlé in the European breakfast cereal market. General Mills brings a unique brand portfolio, production know-how and product development skills; Nestlé its distribution networks and marketing skills in a European context.

Option 3: mergers and acquisitions

Definition
Acquiring an equity stake in a company. Mergers may involve the creation of a new company.

When is it appropriate?

■ when speed of entry is required owing to the dynamics of the market
■ when technology can be acquired along with patents and trademarks

- when creating international brands with home market potential
- when the industry dynamic is such that rapid expansion is required to survive
- when competitor advantages can be neutralized
- when economics of scale convey advantages.

Matrix position (Figure 5.2)

- as part of ongoing strategic development.

Things to watch out for

- Hostile acquisition may be difficult in certain markets due to difficulty in obtaining accurate financial data.
- Political repercussions are always possible, both at home and in the prospect's market.
- Offensive defence – the acquirer itself becomes the target of an acquisition. MCI in the US telecoms market was planning a merger with BT, but instead was swallowed by a US rival, World Com.
- Managing the takeover. Combining and integrating the companies will have substantial repercussions for morale. There must be a corporate and cultural 'fit'.
- Be ready to move and move fast as targets become available.
- Don't buy in haste; be sure it is a central component of long-term corporate strategy.
- Don't pay over the odds.

Making it work

- Use professional advisors.
- Understand your acquisition's basis for doing business; what values are you buying into?
- Ensure there is a match in terms of skills, resources and cultures.
- Exchange managers.
- Evaluate and take strong decisions.
- Communicate the vision, share values, drive from the top and give people something to buy into.
- Incorporate the merger/organization into the strategic plan and do it quickly.
- Have a strong central team committed to success.

- ■ Engage in task force management using all available resources.
- ■ Take the shareholders with you – there must be a financial logic.
- ■ Long-term corporate marketing will fuel the firm's ability to adopt this strategy.

Example
PepsiCo's entry into Poland began with a joint venture with Wedel, a long-established Polish confectioner. PepsiCo brought its brands, while Wedel brought its distribution and reputation.

British Airways and American Airlines are currently pursuing a 'merger' of their transatlantic and US flights.

Cadbury entered the European market through the acquisition of Hueso in Spain and Poulain in France.

Philip Morris established a global presence in the food market through the acquisition of General Foods, Kraft and Jacob Suchard. This facilitated a move away from the tobacco business.

Option 4: green field development

Definition
The establishment of a new operating facility in an overseas market.

When is it appropriate?

- ■ when local know-how is unavailable, especially in emerging markets
- ■ when governments will incentivize activity (ie pay 'golden hello' grants)
- ■ when the product has patent protection
- ■ when there is an opportunity to create the market in the image of the company
- ■ when there is low environmental risk
- ■ when capital is available
- ■ when establishing new operations is easier than changing existing operations.

Matrix position (Figure 5.2)

- ■ low risk
- ■ high opportunity
- ■ high control.

Things to watch out for

■ Be confident that a sustainable and profitable market exists over time.
■ Potential expropriation of assets as a result of political change.
■ Cultural fit between the management and work practices of the home and host markets.
■ Management effort required is substantial
■ Control and communication are sometimes difficult and must be planned for and managed.
■ Local skills and infrastructure must exist or be created.
■ Local law relating to all aspects of business.
■ What is the potential for international marketing from this new base?

Making it work

■ Local acceptance is crucial.
■ Managing the environment over the long term will be the key to success. Political lobbying and public relations will be essential parts of the mix.
■ Ensure that capital commitment is managed. Manage the project in its entirety.

Examples

■ Toyota and Nissan in the UK car market
■ Siemens in the UK
■ McVitie's in China
■ Unilever in China

Option 5: strategic alliances

Definition

Two or more companies whose global goals are compatible combine formally or informally to develop their value chain activities in order to sustain and/or achieve significant competitive advantage. There is no equity exchange and the alliance is managed by agreement.

They represent a variety of cooperative arrangements from marketing through to R&D across all aspects of the value chain. The aim is to develop critical competencies. Strategic alliances may be used at all stages of international development and can be used to support activity at all strategic levels of involvement. Competitors will often combine their talents at the R&D level to provide technological breakthroughs which can then be exploited separately (eg a number of high-tech companies collaborated in the development of flat screen television monitors).

When is it appropriate?

■ when there is a concentration of businesses in mature markets. Alliances allow the dynamics of the market to be managed
■ in high-risk markets with a high cost base

■ when resources are not available to develop, sustain and support a technology breakthrough by the individual firm.
■ when access is sought to problem markets
■ alliances can establish standards and provide valuable barriers to entry to potential competitors
■ when it is advisable to spread the risk of investment in new processes, products and markets
■ to provide a regional presence
■ when collaboration and cooperation will create added value for customers and for the partners
■ to defend the home market from aggressive penetration from outside
■ to block competitor activity in overseas markets
■ to spread the cost of R&D.

Matrix position (Figure 5.2)

■ appropriate at all levels and stages of activity.

Things to watch out for

■ Exclusivity should be demanded where appropriate.
■ Strategy may end up being driven by competitors.
■ Ensure cooperation yields market-based benefits for both or all parties.
■ Define the business and look for complementarity in the partners' business definition. Combine to add value to the market offering.
■ Ensure that key areas of advantage are not compromised.
■ In a dynamic environment alliances must be able to change, evolve and die without major problems being created.

Making it work

■ Choose the right partner.
■ Look for strategic complementarity.
■ Look for value added in the eyes of the market/customer.
■ Negotiate the extent of cooperation.
■ Include an exit strategy.
■ Cover all outcomes via contract.
■ Communicate.

Examples

■ The new Swatchmobile city car in a collaboration between Swatch and Mercedes-Benz.
■ Disney and McDonald's cooperate over merchandising.
■ Airbus is the result of a pan-European strategic alliance, as is the Eurofighter military jet.

ELECTRONIC DISTRIBUTION

Man plus information plus software is greater than man plus information

(*Stan Rapp*)

The development of a global communications network through satellite communications has developed a new means of market entry.

The Internet is becoming a valuable means of entry, and for a fraction of the price of traditional methods all companies, irrespective of size, are able to establish a global presence. At present there is a low level of connections. This is particularly the case in private households. Business-to-business markets are better developed, and those who have access are open to consumer offers. (Incidentally, the pace of change is staggering and is such that our computer does not recognize Internet in its spell check menu!)

There are huge opportunities if handled correctly. This is virtual market entry. Through technology, the smallest company can be a global player. The environment in cyberspace is perfect for business: no politics, few legal constraints, and a global society of shared values and language can be accessed for the price of a local phone call. The only borders are in the mind-set. The only limit – imagination. Cyberspace is the borderless world of commerce: a free and liberal trading environment which is truly global.

All businesses must link into and evaluate the viability of the Net. Those who do not risk disappearing. However, there are some difficulties/considerations.

■ The ease of development of Internet sites does create problems for some companies.
■ The Internet may not 'fit' strategically with the current level of operation.
■ How might transactions be managed?
■ Can the customer communicate with you via email or via telephone, and how do you take the order?
■ Can orders be fulfilled, both geographically and legally?
■ Can the firm cope with an influx of demand?
■ There are problems in managing the development of Internet sites. The ease of development means that many companies will have several 'official' sites. This dilutes the company presence on the net and can create confusion in the eyes of the consumer.
■ Companies must begin by defining the business they are in/want to be in. Information and software providers are obviously suited to Internet marketing; others will rely on traditional channels with the Net acting as a new medium of communication but little more. A balance has to be struck.

Companies which have succeed in developing an international presence via the Net include Martindale Hubbel, part of the Reed Elsevier group, who market legal directories via the Net, and Amazon.com, which describes itself as the world's largest bookstore. Amazon can provide access to 2.5 million titles sent by courier worldwide and paid for via credit card. They were reported to have had revenues of 25 million dollars in 1996. 'Products from Florence' (this is the brand name) in Italy is another site that shows how Internet marketing is overtaking traditional strategies. A conglomerate of small regional producers have combined on the net to create a very neat virtual Tuscan arcade which can be accessed globally. Global consumers can browse for leather goods, olive oil and La Perla underwear to create the perfect combination!

EXIT STRATEGIES AND STRATEGIC DEVELOPMENT

Review the strategic space map. Opportunities and risks exist and change over time. Profit optimization, which is the ultimate deciding factor in market entry, will inevitably involve exit or development strategies.

Part of the process of managing the entry process is that exit and development strategies must be incorporated within the international marketing plan.

International strategic choice will reflect the company's level of involvement, and at each level an appropriate exit strategy must be in place to ensure that the business can survive should adverse scenarios develop.

Flexibility is the key, and in a rapidly evolving environment strategic flexibility, which allows for the need to change, adjust and tailor activity is a core advantage.

SUMMARY

The entry strategy defines the rules of engagement in overseas markets. It determines the configuration of all the functional areas of the business. Companies need to be imaginative and bold in the choice of entry strategies. Think the unthinkable; look for cooperation with unlikely collaborators. Ask the question 'What will the market for the product category look like in ten years' time?'. How can you best deliver benefits to your company over time? Can this be done alone? Certainly alliance collaboration and networking would appear to present a way forward, and partners will probably fall outside current industry classification.

Look at your customers carefully. How can *they* create value? How can you help them? If you are in cosmetics, why concentrate on external appearance? What about the inner body or the physical body? For example why isn't the Body Shop looking at meditation, physical education, spiritual development and education? The balance of body and mind is key. Body Shop may in the future look for inspiration or cooperation with functional food producers, information providers and educators.

After all, who would have thought 15 years ago that the owner of a chain of record shops would own an airline? Who would have thought that the owner of an airline would market vodka and cola? Who would have thought that a marketer of vodka could market financial services? Richard Branson's Virgin group has done this and much more, including the latest venture of 'Virgin Active': a new health club chain.

Who would have considered that banking and telecommunications would be so closely linked? Who are tomorrow's bankers? Probably retail organizations and Internet service providers. The cost of establishing an Internet-based bank has been estimated at a mere £1 million. Give careful consideration to how the organization will deliver benefits to your customers in the future. Chapters 5 and 6 are becoming redundant as you read them. The traditional methods of entry are becoming increasingly irrelevant. Why establish distributors when you can manage the Internet? Why give an agent 35 per cent of the price of your product when you can sell direct and create the trust and bond that customers want? Dialogue is the key to loyalty, and loyalty will drive businesses in to the future. Are you ready for the future?

7

What Should we Sell? Product Policy in International Marketing

INTRODUCTION

'Customers buy what we make'. This is the clarion cry of the sales-led company – the type of company that represents all that Levitt (1960) talked about when he described marketing myopia. The company is introspective; it focuses on processes, is remote from its customers and ultimately is almost certainly doomed.

Marketing is about producing that which customers need. In business applications marketing is about making what customers want to buy and understanding that want so well that we do not just satisfy our customers' needs but delight and surprise them time and time again.

The match between the product and the market is ultimately the key to successful business. In international markets this match often needs to be reconsidered. Even those companies who can say with confidence that, in their home market, they do indeed make what customers want to buy, will find that the environment overseas will be different and often will demand a reconsideration of existing practice.

In some cases this is unimportant, but in most the change in the external environment will demand adaptation of the product to achieve a closer fit with the market. This is a very important strategic decision, and the failure to recognize the far-reaching consequences of product adaptation will have serious repercussions. It may be that the product is such that adaptation is unnecessary, but this is highly unusual. In almost all circumstances the transfer of a bundle of unique benefits to customers (the essential task of a product), will need to be adapted to local market conditions in some way. The product must be right and must be appropriate to the nature of local demand.

Adaptation may be expensive, and this must be built into the planning process at an early stage. It may be that some of the costs of adaptation can be offset against penetration of similar markets which require similar adaptation. For example, the introduction of environmentally friendly packaging materials will be appropriate (indeed, may be required by law) in many other markets.

Care needs to be taken; what we are looking at is the balance between adaptation and the cost. We must determine what is essential in the process and what customers may live with. We must achieve a balance between customer and organizational needs.

NATURE OF THE PRODUCT

It is important at this stage to understand the nature of the product. As we have said, a product is a bundle of benefits appropriate to our customers' needs.

The benefit may accrue through the physical characteristics of the product (eg the product performs faster than its rivals). Benefits may be gained from the image of the product (eg I buy Heinz products because I trust the brand or I always buy Nike because my friends admire my choice). Benefits may be gained from the support services which are offered (eg the warranty that Daewoo offers is superb and the after-sales service is excellent). The physical product may not be the state of the art, but differentiation is achieved through service levels that are leading edge.

Consider the following example: I buy mineral water. Mineral water costs 75 pence per litre. Petrol costs 55 pence per litre.

What am I buying when I buy mineral water?

Among other things, I am buying convenience through packaging; a guarantee of purity;a physical product; a lifestyle; a brand (eg Perrier).

It is clear that benefit is gained from a combination of factors, and that meeting basic physical needs is perhaps the easiest of these to reproduce in the international arena. We know that the basic need to drink can be met in many different ways. In the above example, water can be taken straight from the tap. However, increasing numbers of people are prepared to pay more than they pay for petrol for the most plentiful substance on the planet.

In the case of the international marketing of mineral waters we need to consider how terms like purity, convenience and lifestyle are interpreted in the target market and adapt the configuration of benefits to suit the local market. In a market in which competition exists we would need to develop this configuration so that our product occupies a unique position in the mind of the market.

It is possible to view several different dimensions within a product offering (Figure 7.1). The list below provides full details.

Core product	*Core component*
The need that is being met	The physical product
	Functional features
	Technology
The formal product	*Packaging component*
The physical enhancement of the	Design
core product	Packaging
	Quality
	Price
	Branding
	Packaging
The augmented product	*Support services component*
That which enhances the offer	Access
	Repair and maintenance
	Delivery and installation
	Warranty
	Spares
	Branding
	Service levels

It is clear that ultimately satisfaction will depend on the coordination of all these factors and it is equally clear that the new environment into which our product is placed may demand adaptation of each or any of these elements.

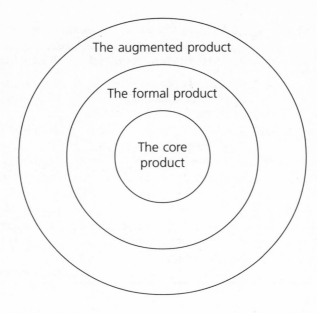

Figure 7.1 *The dimensions within a product offering (Kotler, 1996)*

What is also true is that different markets will place different emphasis within the three levels. In developing for new markets the emphasis may be on the core component, a basic product reflecting local needs and incomes. In mature markets, warranties, services levels and maintenance may be at a premium. Table 7.1 gives an example in the automotive sector.

Any analysis of your own products should take key environmental variables and through them indicate the degree of adaptation required.

MARKETING AUDIT AND THE PRODUCT

The planning process and the accompanying environmental audit is the key to the analysis of the product–market match. This audit will determine the extent to which the product should be adapted. On a broad basis the degree of sensitivity to the market environment will determine the extent to which the product will need to be adapted. The extent of adaptation is crucial for business. Adaptation

Table 7.1 *An analysis of products in the automotive sector*

Environmental factors	Adaptation required	Product level
Legislation	Lean burn engines	Core product
Climate	Air conditioning, heated seats	Formal product
Poor technical support	Simpler design, basic models only	Augmented
Inappropriate brand	New branding	Augmented
Strong safety laws	Stricter technical specifications	Core
High interest rates	Pricing	Augmented
Lower incomes	Quality/price changes	Core/augmented
Spare parts	Ancillary business development	Formal/augmented
Language	Support documentation	Augmented

will add to the cost base of the product and affect the ability to compete in certain markets.

Companies have dealt with this issue by using different strategies. Some companies choose to incorporate added extras as standard rather than adapt from market to market. Others choose to design modular products that can be configured to any customer's requirements, but again this modularity is standardized. For example, Iveco produces a wide range of modular components for its range of trucks, sufficient, it believes, to compete in the global market.

Czinkota shows the relationship between market and product adaptation (Figure 7.2). However, on a macro basis the characteristics and the structure of the industry may determine the extent of the necessary adaptation. We can see below that while there are substantial pressures in the telecomms sector towards globalization, at the local level there remains a need to adapt the marketing mix.

Despite this, as the pressures at corporate and operational level are worked out we can see the beginnings of a standardized approach even to local marketing. For example, BT's Friends and Family discount scheme was originally developed in the USA by MCI. The success of the programme in the USA was such that MCI gained seven percentage points in the market, and this has led to MCI becoming a potential world player in this market. While Friends and Family in the UK is the same concept as in the USA, the style and execution are, of course, adapted to meet local needs and market

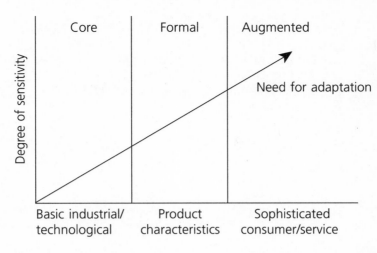

Figure 7.2 *The relationship between market and product adaptation (Czinkota and Ronkainen, 1995)*

conditions. As Figure 7.3 shows, standardization may not always be possible or desirable.

The drive, however, is towards standardization where possible. This has to be the preferred option, simply because it manages margins and drives down costs, enabling companies to set low prices when the market demands it. Those companies that can drive down costs can gain real market advantage. Brand leadership in international markets is yielding marketing margin, enabling and consolidating brand positions as well as creating the ability to charge a premium. There is a virtuous circle at work.

There are a number of other factors which are driving standardization.

▨ Economies of scale in production and other systems.
▨ Consumer mobility – your product will be seen in any number of international markets.
▨ Technology is driving the process and is creating global markets and the ability to reach these markets.
▨ Communication and information are becoming homogeneous and increasingly systems support standard solutions.
▨ Reducing barriers to trade, deregulation, etc.
▨ The country of origin effect may encourage standardization.

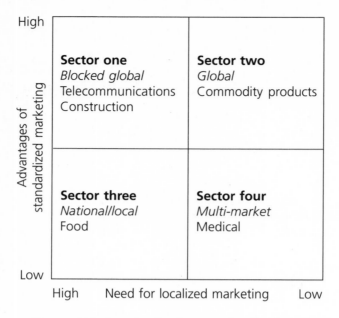

Figure 7.3 *Standardized versus localized marketing*

■ Market convergence – the emergence of global sectors, regional markets and the strategic role of the Triad economies of Europe, Japan, south-east Asia and North America.

Most of these factors tend to be organizationally and supply side driven, and they must be set against customer- and market-driven factors, which include the following.

■ Culture: does the use of the product offend tradition? Are there cultural taboos surrounding the marketing of the product? Language, morality and media dynamics may affect our communications message (for example, the furore surrounding Benetton's advertising).
■ Differences in customer tastes. The leading confectionery brands in south-east Asia tend to be sugar-based and are often medicated. The storage of chocolate products in high temperatures is difficult and the stronger flavours suit local tastes.
■ Differences in behaviour
  – Biscuits in the Italian market are often eaten at breakfast.
  – Ideas of status; what constitutes conspicuous consumption?
  – What constitutes 'youth' culture, is it a driving force in the market?

- Is 'traditional' in vogue, or is 'modern' a driving force?
▓ Government factors. Environmental legislation may affect our
 product specification (eg rulings on CFC content in aerosol sprays).
▓ Consumption patterns.
 - Patterns of purchase
 - Is the product purchased at the same rate?
 - Is it purchased by the same income group/segment?
 - How is the purchase decision made? Who dictates brand choice
 in the overseas market?
 - Who is the key decision maker?
▓ Usage patterns
 - Is the product used for the same purpose?
 - Is the product used in different amounts?
 - Is the method of preparation the same?
 - Is the effectiveness of the product dependent on other products?
 - Does it complement different consumption occasions?
▓ Attitudes towards the brand
 - Is the brand name equally known and acceptable?
 - Are brand values replicable?
 - Is the brand's heritage transferable?

BALANCING CUSTOMER AND ORGANIZATIONAL NEEDS

It is clear from Figure 7.4 that we should assess the need to adapt against the level of opportunity in the market. It costs money to adapt, and the extent of adaptation may force us to reconsider the level of involvement in the market.

There are examples of compromise, and the extent to which adaptation takes place is a corporate decision based on the allocation of resources to identified opportunities. Ferrero, the Italian confectioner, for example, chooses to standardize its European advertising. The 'Ambassador' advertisement has become notorious as a 'Euro' advertisement, but this type of creative execution has not adversely affected Fererro's sales in the market.

Other Euro advertisements perform equally well. Osram, Herta Frankfurters and Dove soap have all adopted a standardized approach to communication. A decision has been taken which recognizes a weaker 'match' with local markets but offsets this through the substantial savings that can be made through centralized production, etc., which recognizes the company's objectives and

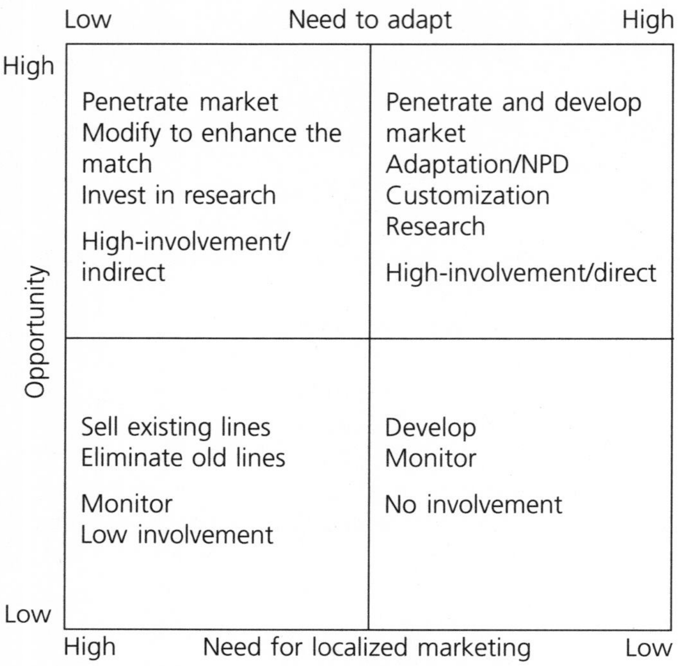

Low   Need to adapt   High

High

| Penetrate market Modify to enhance the match Invest in research High-involvement/ indirect | Penetrate and develop market Adaptation/NPD Customization Research High-involvement/direct |

Opportunity

| Sell existing lines Eliminate old lines Monitor Low involvement | Develop Monitor No involvement |

Low

High   Need for localized marketing   Low

Figure 7.4 *Adaptation versus opportunity matrix*

deals with the need to communicate effectively, although perhaps in a suboptimal way. In fact, the adaptation of the communications message supporting the product is a cost-effective way of changing the perception of the product as a whole. Figure 7.5 is a useful way of considering the role of communications in the product mix.

Global strategy almost certainly will involve some adaptation. Examples of global players include McDonald's and the cola producers. The extent to which even these common examples can be called globally standardized is certainly debatable. Coca-Cola changes its recipe to account for changes in taste, while McDonald's will change its product mix to account for local taste, as we saw in the movie *Pulp Fiction*. In Newcastle they even allow their staff to add the word 'Pet' to their welcome to customers!

It is important, however, to realize that the issues we are dealing with are strategic. Adaptation at the augmented and formal level of the product, in terms of levels of service, etc. will change; however, the positioning and the core product remain the same in a standardized strategy.

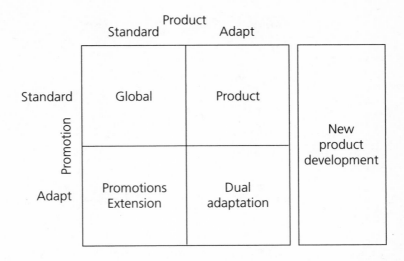

Figure 7.5 *Product and communication adaptation and standardization*

A promotion extension strategy will suit a company producing a standard product, but which requires a local interpretation. Products with different local use patterns will require communications to reflect this.

Product adaptation using standard communication is used in many markets. Product specifications may be forced to change because of local regulations or other factors in the marketing environment. Beer may be brewed to a different strength, be packaged differently or served at different temperatures, for example.

Adaptation of both communications and product demands a high strategic level of involvement and a high level of opportunity in the market. It demands customization and a high and sustained level of return. It is also a more often used strategy in markets where there is a high service element. Because of the essential characteristics of services, an intangible, heterogeneous product is easier to adapt.

THE INTERNATIONAL PRODUCT LIFE CYCLE (PLC)

The PLC as a tool for marketing strategy decisions has been over-used and abused and to some extent discredited over the last 10 years. In the international arena the international PLC can still help in the analysis of appropriate entry methods and the selection of markets, and importantly can act as a guide to international portfolio analysis.

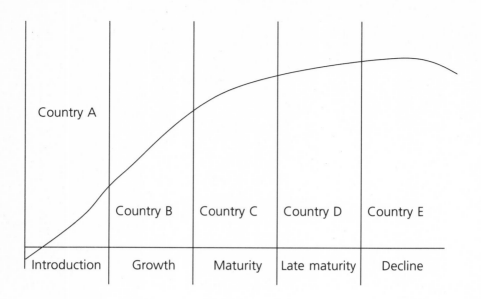

Figure 7.6 *The international product life cycle*

The international diffusion of new products is an important consideration in the overall generation of revenue for any business operating overseas. When Volkswagen stopped production of the Beetle in Europe production was carried on in Mexico. As products enter their late maturity in the home market, for example, they might well be in a launch phase in overseas markets (Figure 7.6). In this way we can maximize revenue over the international life of the product.

Extreme examples include hand-powered sewing machines in Africa and outmoded PCs in developing countries. One recent winner of the Queen's Award for Export Achievement went to a company specialising in marketing second-hand clothing in the developing world.

There is less potential for this type of life cycle extension as the pace of change accelerates and technological diffusion speeds up. Developing countries are less inclined to accept inferior products.

THE COUNTRY OF ORIGIN EFFECT

An important consideration in international product development is the country of origin effect. In certain markets this is important, and the global or international player has an advantage in that it is able to select the preferential country of origin.

It is interesting to note that the requirement for 'Made in' to be included on imports into the UK was originally established to protect the British consumer from substandard products made in Germany. Of course, made in Germany now implies many things, but usually not poor quality!

Recent research carried out in Hungary tried to encourage Hungarian consumers to compare different countries to animals – Britain was regarded as a 'sleek racehorse'. In certain product sectors this may be an advantage, and a company with production in say the UK and Russia would almost certainly choose to import from the UK, all other things being equal.

Of course, country of origin may be implied and equally obscured by trade marks and brand names. Berghaus outdoor clothing is made not in the testing conditions of the Arctic Circle but in Cumbria. Land's End is an American mail order business, as is Racing Green. Clausthaler alcohol-free lager, made in England, could not be further away from its implied German roots.

BRANDING

Product branding is dealt with in more detail under communications, but branding is an essential part of the product specification; it ties in closely with the key areas of positioning and product perception. Gold Blend coffee is lent something beyond its role in the instant coffee market, through association with the word Gold. Gold implies something beyond the physical characteristics of the product and enhances the core proposition. The use of Gold, implying luxury, is something that may well translate perfectly in international markets, but other brand names are not so readily transferable, and in an age when global branding is a key area for development brand names need careful research and testing.

For example, 'GPT' in France, when read quickly, translates as 'I have farted'; 'Young's' in China means 'sexually vigorous'; and 'MR2' in France reads as 'M R Deux', which again has an unfortunate meaning.

There are hundreds of examples in this area. Some appeal to the childish sense of humour in us all, and equally appealing is the element of *Schadenfreude*. These are, after all, mistakes, some of which cost a fortune to put right.

The rules for international brand transfer are:

■ translate and back translate
■ look for double meanings
■ provide a country of origin cultural reference point if required
■ use a consultant
■ take legal advice.

SUMMARY

In this chapter we have looked at the need to define carefully the product market match. The product should be made up of the bundle of satisfactions demanded by the customer. The interpretation of these satisfactions is made at three levels: the core product, the formal product and the augmented product. It is usually easier to adapt at the augmented and formal level than at the core level.

In establishing the extent of adaptation in international markets we must evaluate the level of opportunity against customer needs and the resources and requirements of the organization.

We can use the international PLC in certain markets to assess the management of the international product portfolio.

We must assess the impact of the country of origin effect and configure the international mix to exploit the opportunities that this may offer.

The connections between marketing communications and branding and the product must be established, and this is dealt with in the chapter on marketing communications.

The product–market match is the first of the stages in meeting customer requirements.

8

What Should we Charge?

INTRODUCTION

Pricing is the only area of the marketing mix that raises revenue for the organization. All other activities are costs. Successful pricing is therefore a key element in the management of the marketing mix.

Pricing is often neglected by marketing managers, who prefer to deal with the more 'glamorous' areas of the mix, such as new product development (NPD) or communications. This means that this key area is often ignored, relegated to a lower strategic level or left to the last minute.

Price is often the first point of comparison for customers evaluating your product against the competition. But price is not the only point of difference. Pricing decisions need to be built into and considered within the planning process; indeed, pricing is a highly strategic activity. If we are not to engage simply in cost-plus pricing then this must be recognized.

Equally important is the fact that purchase decisions are not just based on price. Past relationships, service levels, response times, etc. may assume equal or higher importance in the mind of the consumer. Price therefore needs to be considered as a part of the total package of benefits offered to customers.

In international markets the pricing decision becomes more complex. The marketing environment changes, the expectations of customers are different and we have to deal with the mechanics of pricing in a foreign currency and the handling of foreign currency transactions. In addition, the cost base of international business is difficult to analyse.

The problem of allocating costs to export marketing has to be considered, as must the problem of accounting for depreciation of overseas assets. All these areas distract from the key point, which is that unless your price is competitive, or other elements of the offer attract a premium, business will be difficult.

PRICING STRATEGIES

On entering the international arena, companies first need to take the decision as to what strategy they will follow when setting a price in the market. There are three broad alternatives: market skimming, market penetration and what the market will bear.

Market skimming

This strategy is normally associated with unique products with a sustainable point of differentiation in the market. This will attract a premium price. The objective is to maximize revenue and profit before serious competition emerges. The amount of profit available from this strategy will reflect the ability of the company to sustain and develop this point of difference. In certain sectors it may be appropriate for a very short period; in others with trade mark or patent protection, skimming may be sustained for years.

This strategy is also particularly suited to niche products, which target customer needs more precisely and are tailored to meet those needs, again attracting a premium.

Innovative products and new-to-market products also have the advantage of giving the company the ability to set the price benchmark for the industry. The introduction of the Sony Walkman is a good example of this.

Skimming is not necessarily selected on the basis of a high cost base. Indeed, those companies with the lowest cost bases have been seen to set the highest prices in the market. Price is not necessarily a function of cost, but reflects the position the company wishes to adopt in the market. Market leaders are not always volume producers — they are usually innovators, and can attract higher unit prices which yield greater margins.

Market penetration

This reflects the setting of a low price to gain rapid penetration of the market. This may be for several reasons:

▨ to deter other entrants into the market by establishing price as a barrier to entry
▨ to enter markets quickly to lock customers in
▨ to establish volume to cover costs of production
▨ to generate maximum revenue from short-term opportunities
▨ to utilize assets to their full extent
▨ to reduce the marginal costs of production.

This strategy does not encourage differentiation, and a cost-based strategy implied by penetration is often a hard position to defend if advantage is simply based on low price.

In international markets low-cost producers are emerging each day in many countries. The cost competitor from hell is just around the corner. Sustainable advantage via low pricing may be sustained through consolidation and volume, but it is always a vulnerable position. If there is any other advantage then it should attract a premium.

The assumption is that lower prices will increase sales. This is rarely true.

What the market will bear

This is appropriate for companies that have, and can sustain, a point of differentiation. This may rely on the bundle of benefits encapsulated by the total market effort and the configuration of core formal and augmented product factors. The key point is that the differentiation is clear and sustained. The following factors may provide this:

▨ relative uniqueness of the product
▨ sustained brand position
▨ company reputation
▨ skill in managing the marketing mix
▨ managing selective channels of distribution
▨ managing the communication mix
▨ database activity and information-based strategies.

Other considerations include:

▪ likely volumes
▪ company and product cost base
▪ required ROI
▪ the state of the industry life cycle.

This strategy is also appropriate when it is difficult for the end user to make comparisons in the local market-place. For example, in circumstances where the initial price is a small proportion of the total expenditure (such as in mobile phone marketing) the cost of the set may be negligible but the ongoing connection charges are high. In services like accounting and consultancy it is hard to compare prices, as is also the case with other intangible service-based products.

GLOBAL PRICING STRATEGIES

For well-developed international players who operate in several markets there is an additional dimension: the need to manage price across diverse international markets. This is a major issue in regional markets like the EU, where harmonization of tax regimes and the development of a single market means price parity and ease of comparison, and where there are problems with parallel importing and the development of unofficial channels.

Managing the process: planning for price

Price should be developed as part of the international planning process. Price levels should reflect the nature of the business and the overall revenue/profit objectives for the organization. It is a long-term strategic process which must be sustained over time. Price must be seen as inextricably linked to the company's profit goals and objectives.

After the overall consideration of objectives we consider the strategic alternatives discussed above. At the next level we look at the pricing environment in local, regional or global markets, depending on the business definition. We develop a tactical approach to pricing in local markets which may include discounting policy, the cost of financing and warranty provision. The area of finance for purchase is an area of business which may in itself be profitable, be developed through local requirements, or equally be developed as a differentiator in the market. GUS and Ford make more money from financing their deals than from selling the original product.

The key area in local markets is to consider the likely competitive response. Established companies will not sit quietly and watch an attack on their markets. They are entrenched and they have a profit stream; you do not. They can engage in discounting and put pressure on or incentivize key intermediaries to destock your product. If you are going to enter the market, how will you handle this response? How long can you sustain the battle? How long can your competitors sustain the battle? What core advantage do you have?

Development of the export price

The dynamics of setting a price in international markets are complex. For the multinational or global player there are additional factors to consider. These are dealt with at the end of the section. Here we look at the process for SMEs.

Cost of adaptation

We must take into account the additional cost of modifying the product for overseas customers in terms of fixed and variable costs, for example:

■ the cost of changes to machine parts
■ the cost of changing formulation (eg outlawed ingredients)
■ changes in product format (perhaps the size of the product)
■ changes in packaging format (eg from PET bottles to glass)
■ changes in labelling to incorporate languages and local regulation.

Operational and logistics costs

Here we must take into account the following.

■ The additional cost of packaging for transportation by sea and air. The product must survive long journeys and we cannot assume smooth roads!
■ Additional packaging for security to prevent pilferage and product tampering. The packaging must also prevent damage in open-air storage in hostile climates.
■ Additional warehousing and inventory costs. You must be able to supply anticipated demand. Long runs are more profitable than short runs. Can you anticipate demand and produce and store more profitably than producing via short runs?

■ The cost of delivery, insurance and administration.
■ What control and planning procedures are in place to take account of the potential increase in the price charged by key intermediaries?

The management of the cost base at this level may be demanded by customers. Equally, costs incurred in this area may be designed to enhance the product offer. The needs of the customer and the ability to pay should drive the management planning process.

Costs of entering the market
These include:

■ tariffs
■ taxes
■ Other government influences and constraints. How are prices seen by the government? Are they seen as reasonable or as exorbitant? Are prices controlled locally?

Areas of concern include the pharmaceuticals sector, where in certain markets governments are condoning the import of counterfeits to ensure supply.

Commercial risks must be covered. The process of getting paid needs to be considered, and possibly insured. Export credit cover is expensive, and letters of credit must be costed.

Currency fluctuations must be accounted for. These include the costs of hedging, running foreign current accounts and handling complex transactions.

Marketing costs
Research and market investigation via in-house or external agencies will be expensive, as will market visits.

The evaluation and establishment of intermediaries may involve many visits to the market. Regular communication will be expensive and will involve regular face-to-face meetings.

The cost of promotion (trade fairs, publicity material and other marketing communications materials) must be accounted for.

The cost of export negotiations
In certain markets negotiations will take much longer. In Japan and China, for example, the decision-making process is generally longer.

The etiquette of negotiation needs careful management, and this again may mean additional costs.

Human resources and organizational costs
These include:

▓ the costs of people in production, process, delivery and logistics
▓ the cost of establishing an export department or managing the export process
▓ the use of consultants and the purchase of other expertise out of house
▓ hiring temporary labour.

Additional management time will be diverted from the home market; therefore more people may be required to be employed for the home market operation.

The cost of finance
There are substantial cash implications. Suitable financing must be set up before orders are received. It is possible to go broke with a full order book.

The need for price stability
Despite the apparent complexity of the cost base, end users and intermediaries require stability in pricing structures. Therefore it is imperative that the cost base is established and pricing levels reflect the possible changes in its constituent elements.

The net effect of all this is that the price in the export market may be higher than the price in the home market for most SMEs. You must be sure that your price in international markets is sustainable as your cost base escalates. You must ensure that as this cost base expands you can achieve an acceptable margin on activity.

Factors to consider

▓ Are you meeting customer needs?
▓ Are you perceived as producing advantage for your customers? Do you have niche status? What is the basis of this status?
▓ Are you special, and is this difference sustainable over time? Special today must mean special tomorrow.
▓ Frequency of purchase: a one-off high-value purchase may sustain a premium position.

- Level of comparability. If your product is readily comparable with local alternatives you may not be able to command a premium.
- Is the country of origin effect working for you?
- Are your service standards capable of replication in overseas markets? Many companies will buy on delivery targets rather than price.
- You must ensure that, where possible, the additional cost incurred in international activity adds value in the eyes of the customer. Use logistics and delivery as a sustainable advantage. This may even allow you to increase margins.

TERMS OF TRADE AND METHOD OF PAYMENT

Price negotiation

Price is the focus of most negotiations and is inevitably the most sensitive. Price must be approached from the point of view of a total package. The negotiation on price must be based around the full range of benefits delivered through the deal. We must be able to compare like with like. Each element must be recognized and its role in price setting should be established before negotiation begins.

Terms of the sale

The standard definitions for the terms of sale are laid down by the International Chamber of Commerce. Incoterms provide a standard format for the framing of international transactions. The current Incoterms were introduced in 1990. The most common are described below.

Ex-works (factory, warehouse, etc)
Prices quoted ex-works apply at the point of origin, literally ex-works, or as they leave the point of origin. The seller agrees to make the product available to the buyer at a specified date or within a specified period. Purchasers acquire the product at the lowest price and can negotiate their own insurance and transportation arrangements.

Free carrier (FCA)
FCA (also named Inland Point), applies only at a designated inland shipping point. The exporter is responsible for loading the product,

but the purchaser must cover all other expenses. If a port of exportation is named the cost of transport is included to the named port.

Free alongside ship (FAS)
The exporter quotes a price that covers transport alongside a vessel at the port of exportation. The seller covers the cost of wharfage and unloading at the dock; the buyer covers all other expenses. The contract will name a specified vessel.

Free on board (FOB)
The exporter covers the cost and insures the risk of transport up to the point that the goods are moved onto the vessel. FOB contracts may specify the port of exportation and the name of the vessel or domestic carrier.

Cost and freight
The exporter covers the cost of transport to the port of importation. The cost of insurance is left to the buyer.

Cost insurance and freight (CIF)
The contract covers the cost of transporting the product to the port of importation. The exporter also covers the risk associated with the transfer of the product. The exporter can gear up the cost of transport and the deal may be more profitable.
Costs include:

- ■ port charges
  - unloading
  - wharfage
  - handling
  - storage
  - cartage
  - lifting
  - demurrage
- ■ documentation charges
  - Certificate of Origin
  - certification of invoices, etc.
  - weight certificates
  - customs documentation
- ■ others
  - transport costs
  - insurance premiums.

Delivered duty paid (DDP)
As implied, the exporter delivers to a specified point (usually the buyer's premises) and covers all costs, including duty and taxes.

Delivered duty unpaid
As above, but the seller does not take responsibility for duty and tax.

The key point about Incoterms is that they can give advantage to the international buyer. Inclusive contracts allow more control and can add value to the offer. Control may ensure that the goods arrive on time, in peak condition and administration is cut down.

Inclusive contracts avoid the risk of misunderstanding, which is very easy in negotiations of this type. Exporters with substantial activity may be able to achieve a very competitive price for transportation and will understand procedures better than many casual importers. This again adds value and differentiates our offer from the competition.

Conversely, for the small volume exporter the use of ex-works pricing may work equally well. Transportation can be left to the buyer or subcontracted to freight forwarders.

THE MECHANICS OF THE DEAL

The mechanics of export are extremely involved. The key point is to ensure that we receive payment for our product. There are a number of additional factors to consider in foreign transactions, and these include:

■ the risk of war or terrorist activity
■ natural disasters
■ government action on debt rescheduling, etc.

These apply above and are in addition to the normal risks which are a part of doing business. A thorough audit as part of the planning process should enable appropriate action to be taken to reduce risk or to cover the company's exposure.

The basic methods of payment for international goods have been designed to attempt to satisfy both the buyer and the seller. The diversity of transactions means that the relative attractiveness of these methods will vary. The main objective has to be to meet the customer's needs without damaging the exporter's position.

The exporter should evaluate the risks, taking into account:

▩ the status and strength of the relationships and the importance of the customer
▩ the size of the deal
▩ the environment in the importing country
▩ competitors' activity
▩ industry practice
▩ the capacity to manage the financial exposure.

The most attractive condition for the exporter is obviously cash before delivery in the exporter's currency. This is not widely used.

Letter of credit

A letter of credit is an instrument issued by a bank at the request of a buyer. The bank promises to pay an agreed amount of money on presentation of documentation specified in the letter of credit, usually the bill of lading, consular invoice and a description of the goods.

Letters of credit are commonly used as they provide advantages for both the buyer and the seller. Figure 8.1 shows the process of transacting via letter of credit.

Letters of credit are classified in three ways.

▩ Irrevocable and revocable: an irrevocable letter of credit cannot be amended or cancelled. All letters of credit are irrevocable unless specified.
▩ Confirmed or unconfirmed: confirmed via a bank. The safest method for the exporter is a confirmed irrevocable letter of credit. Unconfirmed letters of credit simply imply that an advisory role is played by the bank.
▩ Revolving or non-revolving: non-revolving letters of credit are valid for one transaction only. Most letters of credit are non-revolving.

Other payment methods

Documentary collection

The exporter ships the goods, and the documents and draft demanding payment are presented to the buyer through the bank acting as the seller's agent. Time drafts allow for payment in 30, 60 or 90 days

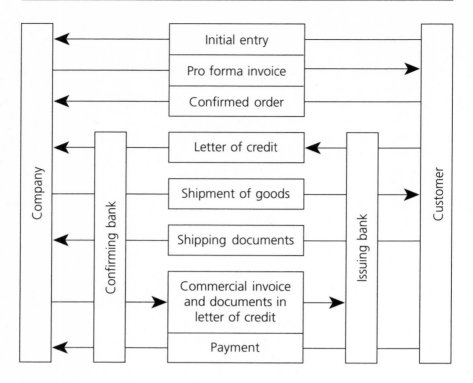

Figure 8.1 *Buying using a letter of credit*

and may be sold at a discount for immediate cash. Sight drafts demand payment on presentation.

Banker's draft
This is drawn by the exporter on the importer. It is similar to a personal cheque.

Open account
The seller assumes a greater amount of risk, as there is no documentation outlining the customer's responsibility. This is the normal manner of transacting in the home market. In the overseas market it removes barriers to business, and this may be advantageous; however, if there is a perceived risk of non-payment other methods are more secure.

Consignment selling
The exporter retains title until sale is made. This is simply a type of sale or return. Payment is deferred until the goods are sold.

Summary of trends

The decision must be based on the following:

- ■ the assessment of risk
- ■ the closeness to the customer
- ■ the frequency of transaction.

Figure 8.2 summarizes the risks and benefits of the various payment methods.

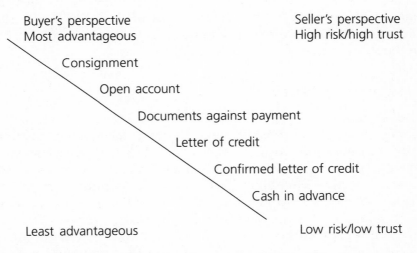

Buyer's perspective
Most advantageous

Seller's perspective
High risk/high trust

Consignment

Open account

Documents against payment

Letter of credit

Confirmed letter of credit

Cash in advance

Least advantageous

Low risk/low trust

Figure 8.2 *Risks and advantages of various methods of payment*

CURRENCY ISSUES

The problems of dealing in foreign currencies are also a major addition to the complexities of managing the international transaction. It is easy for exporters to price in their home currency, but this is rarely acceptable to the buyer, and inevitably currency has to be considered. When currency transactions are managed well then beneficial shifts in exchange rates can produce additional profit, although of course the company should not rely on this source of income. The uncertainty in currency markets is a major problem for businesses planning involvement in markets. While in mature economies there is more stability, and major problems like Britain's withdrawal from the ERM are rare, in developing markets there are more problems.

The process of managing transactions in a foreign currency is demanding and may involve forward buying of currency.

There are two ways of minimizing the risk of adverse currency fluctuations.

■ Negotiate shorter payment terms.
■ Agree a future rate with the bank.

The current debate surrounding the single European currency and the introduction of the Euro is already having practical implications for all European businesses. From 1 January 1999, companies can quote and pay in both their domestic currency and in Euros. This ultimately will reduce the uncertainty of currency transactions, but in the short term it will cause problems.

Alternatives to money

Countertrade

Countertrade is the process where payment for goods is made in part or in full in the form of other goods. It is particularly suitable for markets where there is a shortage of foreign currency or the currency is non-convertible. Tariff and other political barriers can also be surmounted in this way. This means that new markets can be developed, particularly in high-risk markets.

There are problems in handling the countertraded products, as they will almost certainly fall outside the company's area of expertise. Negotiations will also be complex and the contract is difficult to evaluate and control.

Nevertheless, a flexible approach to countertrade and the use of the numerous expert services offered in this field can create additional profits for the company.

Leasing

This is a very important area for capital goods and a major area of opportunity. It ties buyers into the company and creates valuable opportunities for ongoing relationships and cross- and up-selling.

Many companies in this area are forming valuable partnerships that sustain profitable business and help to eliminate the risks of international business.

BROADER ISSUES

Transfer pricing

Those companies with operations in more than one country will have an additional factor to consider in international pricing. The pricing of sales to other companies or divisions within the company can yield substantial benefits.

- It can increase price competitiveness in the international markets.
- It can reduce international exposure to tariffs and taxes.
- It minimizes risks due to currency fluctuation.
- It can help to ease problems in the repatriation of revenues.

The problems in transfer pricing include:

- accusations of dumping; there may be political repercussions.
- Conflict between divisions may arise from the desire of local subsidiaries to make profits at the expense of enhanced overall profits for the corporation from transfer pricing.
- Setting the most advantageous price.
- Difficulty in evaluating local performance.

Multi-brand price positioning

Price as an essential component of positioning has been well documented. Price positioning in international markets becomes more complex as, for example, brand image is undeveloped and will not sustain price differentials. The issue for the international player is to produce a position that will sustain pricing strategies. This might be achieved through:

- uniqueness (ie it is difficult to compare alternatives)
- exclusivity: there are no substitutes
- branding
- perceived benefit is high
- usage is determined by a previous purchase and replacements can be priced high (eg computer printers and ink cartridges)
- a very low purchase price.

The experience effect

For major international players the experience effect may come into play. This affects the cost base of the company. Research has shown that the cost of production reduces over time. This, combined with the economies of scale in production and depreciation over a much larger market, can give international players a significant cost advantage in production, which allows for pricing flexibility.

SUMMARY

Price is the only activity which provides revenue; all other activity is a cost. Therefore price is a highly strategic decision and it must take account of the full package of benefits offered to customers.

In international markets we can consider three broad pricing strategies:

■ market skimming
■ market penetration
■ what the market will bear.

We must be able to include all elements of the international costs in our pricing strategy. These include:

■ adaptation
■ operations and logistics
■ entering the market
■ marketing costs
■ export negotiations
■ human resource costs
■ costs of finance.

The key issue is maintenance of price stability, and we must plan to ensure this if required by our customers.

Price should be negotiated carefully. Incoterms help to establish agreed benchmarks for pricing internationally.

The mechanics of pricing include:

■ letter of credit
■ open account

■ banker's drafts
■ consignment selling.

The appropriateness of the method depends on:

■ the status of the customer
■ the size of the deal
■ competitor activity
■ industry practice
■ management skill and experience.

Alternatives to cash include:

■ countertrade
■ leasing.

These methods can open up closed markets and create additional problems. There are advantages and disadvantages in both methods.

Currency issues must be considered and ways of managing fluctuations should be incorporated.

For larger companies, transfer pricing will yield significant advantage, although the internal politics must be handled delicately.

Pricing must reflect the overall international marketing strategy and be derived from the development of the international marketing plan. Crucially, it must support the required strategic level of involvement.

Pricing may be standardized, adapted to local conditions in the market with no coordination, or set globally, recognizing the need to adapt to local market conditions but reflecting and sustaining the company's long-term positioning in the international/global market.

9

Promotion: Marketing Communications – Talking to our Customers

INTRODUCTION

The communications process in international marketing presents a range of challenges for the marketer.

Communication is constrained and defined by culture as well as the external factors operating in the market. We must understand these external factors and we must know our customers so well that the communications message can be understood and interpreted in the right way, so that the correct response is generated. The international arena is littered with examples of inappropriate communication:

- mistranslation: the slogan 'Come Alive with Pepsi' was translated as 'Pepsi raises relatives from the dead' in China
- the numerous examples of double entendre in brand names
- the use of inappropriate images and symbols.

While many of these provide light relief for the knowing international marketing community, they do represent the most blatant examples of waste of the company's scarce resources, or the inability to gear up brand names in the international context.

The positioning of the product in the customer's mind is largely achieved through the communication of the benefits and features that the customer is looking for. These include brand image and identity, as well as the functional attributes of the product. If they did not, our agencies could simply state 'eat beans' or 'drink beer'. Image is all. As soon as we state a brand name, we summon up an image of a way of life and a use for the product, all determined by the message but also by our interpretation of that message.

Offending religious taboos or standards of decency may be serious problems, but equally serious are the misunderstanding of customer's needs and behaviour and miscommunicating our message or positioning. This failure is often far harder to detect and certainly far harder to correct.

This failure can create long-term problems in marketing in the country under consideration. People can forgive a blatant mistake, and controversy may even help to create a niche position, but targeted customers cannot easily reinvent a brand position once it is established.

PROBLEMS IN INTERNATIONAL MARKETING COMMUNICATIONS

Figure 9.1 shows how the message is interpreted. The external environment comes into play at all levels, and affects the international company and intermediaries and customers.

The role of the environmental audits in the planning process is again vital. We must understand the external factors at work, prioritize them and assess their impact on our ability to do business.

As we plan the communications programme and develop our position in the market we develop and configure the marketing mix. This may target end users in a pull strategy, intermediaries in a push strategy, or both sets of customers.

As we send out our message, the interpretation of that message is influenced by the external environment, by the customers' 'black box' and by competing messages in the channel. It is estimated that the average consumer is subjected to around 2000 advertising messages each day, and this clutter will reduce the effectiveness of our own communication.

The relationship between channel intermediaries and end users will also affect the way our messages are perceived and interpreted.

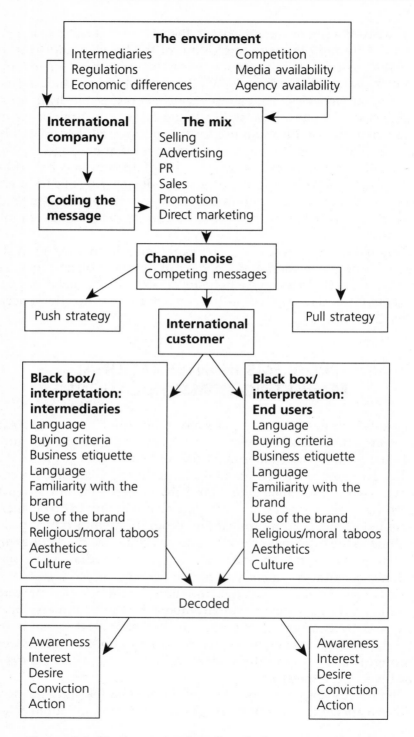

Figure 9.1 *The interpretation of marketing communications*

As the message is interpreted so it results in an outcome. It may raise awareness, create interest, desire or conviction, or result in an action. We hope that this action will be the purchase of our product. The action then should feed back into the communications planning process, a framework for which is shown in Figure 9.2.

A PLANNING FRAMEWORK

Planning for international marketing communications involves the same process as the broad international plan. We must answer the following questions.

■ Where are we?
■ Where do we want to be?
■ How can we best get there?
■ How do we ensure that we arrive?

It is important that we view the communications planning process as part of the overall international plan and that we review our overall strategic intent in the international context.

At the strategic level, many of the questions that the communications plan would need to address will have been answered, for example the broad strategic approach to be followed, the extent of a standardized strategy and the broad targeting and positioning strategy to be adopted in overseas markets. These macro strategies will be predefined as part of the international plan.

An indication of the required return on investment is of course crucial, and the local marketing plan, of which the local communications plan forms a part, will reflect the specific marketing objectives in that market.

Trade fairs, exhibitions and conferences

Trade fairs are an essential element of the international marketing mix.

■ They provide a unique environment in which buyers and sellers interact.
■ They provide useful platforms for product launches.
■ They are invaluable for research.
■ They can be used to test the market for new products.
■ Competitor activity can be monitored.

Review international marketing objectives

Communications objectives across markets

Communications strategy across markets
Standard
Adapted
Segmentation targeting and positioning
Branding

Integration of promotional elements across markets
Trade fairs   Advertising
Personal selling   PR
Sales promotion   Direct marketing

Creative platform across markets
Media choice

Tactical planning within markets
Local objectives
Strategies
Media
Timing

Budgets
Evaluation within market
Contingency within market

Evaluation across markets
Contingency across markets
Feedback to audit

Figure 9.2 *A planning framework*

- They are often used in a business-to-business context.
- They show the product in action.
- Intermediaries can be located.
- The customer comes to you.
- Government-sponsored firms can be a useful point of entry for state contracts.
- They provide a valuable source of leads for the sales force.
- The attendant publicity can be useful.

There are around 2000 trade fairs held annually around the world. Some are standards for the industries that they serve: the Frankfurt book fair, SIAL in France for the food sector, and the toy fair at Earls Court.

Trade fairs and exhibitions should not be viewed as an opportunity for foreign travel. They need to be carefully monitored and evaluated, and objectives should be set to establish success. Your trade association should be able to tell you about the key exhibitions and fairs in your industry.

The government will also help with trade missions, and the DTI will provide details of trade missions and other help available to attend fairs.

Personal selling

Personal selling is often more important than other forms of promotion in international marketing. This occurs for several reasons.

- There may be restrictions placed on other forms of promotional activity.
- Channels are long or markets have very traditional or complex distribution channels.
- Lower wages may enable a sales force to be recruited more effectively.
- Local business etiquette demands it.

Problems in personal selling in the international context

Negotiation style

Approaches to negotiation vary from country to country and are often driven by cultural factors. Pre-visit training and cultural immersion programmes may help your sales force to deal with the context within which negotiations may be carried out.

Other problem areas

■ Pay attention to etiquette and understand the local way of doing business; try not to offend local custom.
■ What is the extent of the relationship? Are your sales people expected to socialize outside the context of the meeting?
■ Are agreements binding? In certain cultures there is a flexible approach to the negotiation process, which is firmed up later.
■ Understand the spoken and silent language of business. While the language of business is English in many cultures, the ability to understand nuances in language may give a substantial advantage to the company. The silent language refers to culturally bound behaviour. What is the culture of gift-giving in business? Are meeting schedules rigorously adhered to?

Recruitment issues

The appointment of the sales force opens up another can of worms for the business: do we recruit locals or an expatriate sales force? Local candidates with product knowledge and appropriate experience may be in short supply, and those which are available may be attracted to locally established enterprises. We also have to consider the following points.

■ How do we train sales people?
■ How do we ensure loyalty?
■ How do we remunerate the sales force? Is commission an acceptable part of the culture?

Expatriate training

The training of the expatriate sales force is essential if it is to have maximum impact. Tone and Walters (1989) have suggested a three-stage approach to training.

■ Initial training
  - length: one week
  - when: prior to departure
  - an introduction to the country or region
  - introduction to the external environment for business
  - introduction to the language
■ Follow-up training
  - length: one month

- when: before departure
- deeper knowledge of attitudes and behaviour
- cultural awareness training
- case study/role-playing approach
■ Immersion training
- length: one month plus
- when: on arrival
- field exercises
- extensive language work
- observation.

Direct marketing and selling

The role of direct marketing is expanding quickly, and direct approaches to selling are occurring in all business sectors around the world. The role of the sales force within a direct marketing organization becomes far more focused and (hopefully) profitable.

Leads generated directly can be analysed and followed up according to their perceived value or potential. The cost of running a sales force is very high. Astute international direct marketing policy can gear up the sales force and shift their role from the largely unprofitable cold calling for acquisition to customer care, management and retention. Compaq, American Express (Amex), Saab, Dell, Visa and Toyota are all examples of companies which have developed direct marketing alongside an existing sales operation. Compaq and Amex have multilingual call centres to deal with enquiries from all over Europe. Dell sells computers directly via a number of different media.

Mail order and catalogue marketing are also having a substantial impact in all sectors, including the business-to-business sector, and this is increasingly international.

The Internet is also having an impact on the way we do business, and the role of the sales force or intermediary is under pressure. Interactivity is allowing the virtual sales force to emerge. This presents unique challenges and opportunities. Dell sells $3 million of computers each day via the Net. The Internet is Toyota's single largest outlet.

The role of the database in allowing the sales force to tap into information about existing or potential customers is also changing the way we do business. The pace of change is staggering.

What is clear is that the pressure towards direct selling will not reduce and the sales force will have to consolidate its role in customer service, and satisfaction and will look to add value to existing customers rather than continually acquire new business.

Sales promotion

Sales promotion is used in a variety of markets and in a variety of ways. Short-term activity designed to achieve an increase in sales of the company's goods or services my be achieved through discounting or through other incentives. This is a highly regulated area and one which causes more difficulty in international markets.

Despite this, sales promotions remain extremely popular, and their use is growing world-wide, in both push and pull strategies. This has been fuelled by the move to database marketing – promotions offer a useful means of data capture for companies.

Advantages of sales promotion

■ tracking effectiveness
■ supporting a brand position
■ incentivizing and rewarding purchase
■ encouraging trial of new products
■ Incentivizing key intermediaries.

Problems in the international arena

■ Regulation. Free prize draws are illegal in Germany, Denmark, Belgium and the Netherlands, among others. The legal environment in this area is a minefield.
■ Problems in sourcing premiums.
■ Making the offer relevant to the local market.
■ Establishing the cooperation of intermediaries for coupon redemption, etc.
■ Lack of infrastructure for EPOS couponing, etc.

Public relations

The communications plan should include public relations activity. It is very difficult to isolate the effects of PR problems in the global market, and plans should be made to deal with problems in one market that may impact on our activity in another.

PR agencies are increasingly able to deal with international clients, and planning and coordination of activity is central to success in this area.

Advertising

Media availability

The expansion of the global media market has been coupled with the consolidation of ownership and the fragmentation of delivery.

The introduction of satellite television and global coverage of certain media procedures gives the international marketer almost unlimited opportunity. MTV, the satellite music station, was held up 10 years ago as one of the driving forces behind the move towards globalization. In fact, MTV today is adding to the pace of fragmentation of consumer markets. MTV offers different programming in Milan and Turin, for example, reflecting local tastes and marketing itself to those different needs. What this means for the companies using the new media to promote their good and services is that there is a range of media available in most markets to support communications strategies, but access to these media will vary, as will response to the message. The regulatory environment which surrounds the media remains nationally determined.

The selection of media will depend on the target audience, access to media and the nature of the product to be promoted. Generally, in developing markets, the use of cinema, radio and posters is more successful than TV and press advertising.

The timing of campaigns needs to be carefully considered. For example, when are the major gift-giving seasons? When do people take vacations?

Regulation

The regulatory environment surrounding the use of advertising remains tight. This means that when using pan-national media the advertiser is constrained and should adhere to the regulations existing in the most regulated country in which the advertisement may appear, or must adapt the advertisement for each market. Regulation in the EU is tight, but according to the rules on commercial messages, advertising that is permitted in one country should be allowed in all other member states. In practice this does not yet occur.

An example of the difficulty created by regulation emerges with Budweiser's sponsorship of the 1998 World Cup in France. Advertising of alcoholic drinks is not allowed in France, and there have been major problems for Anheuser Busch in ensuring that advertising boards may be used in the football grounds. A global event is thus constrained by local rules.

Culture and language

The unwritten regulation of culture also plays a key role in advertising. 'Decent', 'honest' and 'true' are terms which are culturally determined and which vary substantially from country to country.

The tone of voice used in advertising will vary in effectiveness. The British prefer humour, the Americans a direct sell. The standardization of approach may reduce the effectiveness of the message.

The issues of standardization and adaptation are discussed in more detail below.

Standardization vs. adaptation

Much of the debate in recent years in international marketing communications has focused around the merits of standardized against adapted communications strategies. The debate has been on going in this area for many years, but came to the fore in the early part of the 1990s as companies prepared their strategic approach to the single European market. Companies were promised rich returns from the creation of pan-European brands and the consequent economies of scale available at all levels of marketing support, including marketing communications.

There are several key advantages and disadvantages of standardization, listed in Table 9.1.

Figure 9.3, developed by Keegan (1997), shows the strategic decisions regarding promotion as they link with the product decision. This provides a useful framework for assessing options.

Table 9.1 *Advantages and disadvantages of standardization*

Advantages	Disadvantages
Consistency	Not market based, ignores PLC
Cost economy	differences, different usage,
Exploits good ideas to the full	regulation, media, etc.
Easier to control from the centre	Frustrates local managers
Consolidates global position	Local lassitude
Frees management resources	Lost local opportunity
	Problems in replication
	Difficult to manage
	Higher cost of ignoring diversity

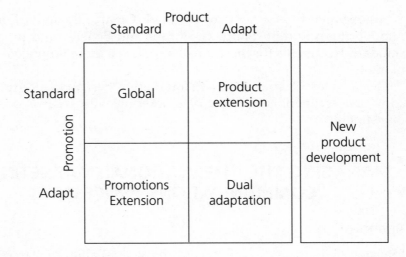

Figure 9.3 *Adaptation and standardization: a framework for strategy*

While the pan-European approach to branding has worked in certain sectors, the problems of managing pan-national communications in Europe remain complex, and very few companies have successfully adopted a pan-national approach to communications planning. Much depends on the nature of the business and the dynamics of the market. In business-to-business markets pan-national communication appears to be more successful than in consumer markets. Culture-free products are relatively more receptive to a standardized approach.

Companies that have adopted a pan-national position will certainly need to adapt their communications programming to local environments. It is possible to use standard execution in, say, TV advertising and adapt using local voiceovers; however, in other areas, for example sales promotion, the law in Europe varies still, and local regulation will demand a change in approach.

What is more important is that research shows that pan-regional approaches tend towards compromise. They lack the real creative hook with which to catch local consumers. Consumers themselves find the creative bland and lacking in humour, and the words 'Euro pap' come to mind!

There are useful approaches to the problem of standardization. One is to produce a range of material and allow out-takes to suit local needs. For example, a 12 minute reel might be produced for a brand and local managers will take out the 30 seconds that best suits the local market.

Sub-regional approaches may also work. Companies divide Europe into Northern Europe, Southern Europe and Benelux and produce standard treatments for these smaller, perhaps more homogeneous, markets.

The answer of course lies in marketing research, pre-testing copy and reconciling the cost of marketing with returns on that investment.

MANAGING THE INTERNATIONAL MARKETING COMMUNICATIONS PROCESS

Agencies

International agencies are increasingly available to carry out standardized or adapted campaigns in overseas markets. Most of the larger groups will be represented in person or through affiliated local agencies in most major markets world-wide. The issue for the company is to decide whether the campaign is best handled centrally or through diverse local organizations.

Domestic agencies
It is usual for most small businesses to use their domestic agency for advice when first moving into international markets. Most smaller agencies will have some international links, but this relationship will need to be re-evaluated as the company expands its international presence.

Appointing local agencies
Recognizing the need for local expertise, some companies will seek to appoint locally based agencies with relevant knowledge, contacts and appropriate skills. These agencies will be coordinated by the company, and the management time required is offset against the local feel of campaigns. This obviously supports a differentiated strategy.

Global agencies
The major agencies will have the ability to coordinate international campaigns and still reflect local differences. The trend to global agencies obviously has certain benefits, but the need for local adaptation due to local conditions means that the small local agency can still have a role to play.

Local agencies still survive for the following reasons.

■ Small is beautiful – local agencies may be creatively hot or have expertise in certain industry sectors.
■ Coordination is not required, due to a highly differentiated strategy or low level of international activity.
■ A high level of activity across the communications mix demands local control and coordination.
■ A local image is vital.
■ The decision is made to employ the best agency in each market and coordinate in-house.

Much depends on the overall level of involvement in international markets and the overall strategic objectives of the company.

Selecting agencies is a demanding and time-consuming task. There are a number of criteria to consider when selecting an international agency.

■ Market and sector expertise: does the agency understand your business and your customers?
■ Country coverage: will the agency be able to travel with you as you develop your international business further?
■ Integration and ancillary support in marketing services: does the company have the ability to provide an integrated campaign across all elements of the promotional mix? Is its planning department geared up for international marketing research
■ What are your own in-company strengths? Does your organization have the skill to carry out any of the work in-house? What services must you buy in?
■ Which of your competitors do they handle?
■ What is their creative reputation?
■ Is the agency familiar with the problems of international coordination? Is the agency able to handle a multi-country brief?
■ What experience does the agency have?
■ What is the image of the agency? Will it support your own image?
■ What is the role of your business in the agency? Have you worked with them in the past?
■ Can you work with these people? Do you know them? Can you get on with them?

The process of selection will take place through three stages.

1. Trawling and the establishment of a short-list. The short-list will be drawn up by reference to the above questions. In addition, you should use personal recommendation, reputation and past experience to establish a short-list of five agencies.
2. Screening. Credentials are presented and a final choice of three agencies may be invited to pitch to a prepared brief.
3. Selection.

SUMMARY

International marketing communications is highly culturally determined.

International marketing communications determines the positioning of the brand and should be carefully considered against the external environment and the dynamics of the market.

The process of planning for international marketing communications is complex and should fit within the international marketing planning process. The strategic decision of cross-market communication needs to be taken before the plan for the local market is established.

The mix for intentional marketing includes:

■ trade fairs
■ personal selling
■ direct marketing
■ sales promotion
■ public relations
■ advertising

We must consider the planning process in the context of media availability, regulation and culture.

Adaptation and standardization must be determined by the market dynamic.

Agencies can help in the management of the communications plan, and the selection of agencies must be handled with care.

10

International Distribution and Logistics

INTRODUCTION

The management of distribution and logistics in the international arena is one of the fastest expanding areas in the marketing mix today.

Wander through the fresh produce section of your local supermarket. Beans from Kenya, broccoli from Ecuador, fish from the West Indies and fruit from South Africa and New Zealand – all fresh, all available 365 days a year at incredibly cheap prices. How? All of this is bought to you via international distribution and logistics.

This is one transparent example of the process in everyday life, but in all areas of business management logistics are driving advantage. Today's customers want the best products at the lowest prices, and they want them now.

We must source globally, taking advantage of low-cost producers and using distribution to close this gap. The distance between the production process and the customer cannot get greater. IT and the management of distribution via flow technology are allowing competitive advantage.

Even small companies no longer rely on local supply. International logistics creates opportunity wherever cost advantages exist and the combination of these advantages can take place anywhere.

It is not just in production that this advantage accrues, but in all elements of the process of delivery – BA manages its ticketing in Mumbai (Bombay). IT is closing the gap between dispersed activity and allowing advantage to be configured globally and delivered locally.

LOGISTICS

Logistics incorporates the design and management of the flow of materials into, through and out of the company.

Logistics is changing rapidly. At the strategic level, the traditional approach has been cost-driven, short-term contracts with anonymous suppliers, designed simply to drive margins on one-off contracts. Today, companies are seeking to gear up this relationship to create additional advantage for customers. They are entering longer term partnerships with suppliers in this area. This allows them to understand the benefit that their customers seek from the arrangement. The integration consolidates the supply chain upstream and downstream, with the company acting as the coordinating factor.

The key to future development is collaboration and coordination to maximize benefits to customers and to ensure higher levels of satisfaction for customers and suppliers. It is the delivery of a win–win situation. This is driven by the idea that benefit may rest not only in price but also in the just-in-time (JIT) delivery of inventory and in environmentally friendly fleet management, all of which can be built into the package of benefits sought by customers.

At the same time collaboration in the production process allows a cost advantage to be gained and offered to the customer if required. This is happening now, to the extent that 35 per cent of all workers on the production line at Mitsubishi Motors are not Mitsubishi employees.

In the USA 40 per cent of material delivery is made on a JIT basis.

The pressures on the value chain are now largely concentrating downstream of the producer. The role of intermediaries in logistics and the management of distribution is becoming an area in which companies can begin to rationalize. The efficient use of freight forwarders can cut out intermediaries, whose role was to get the product in front of the customer. This can be done via catalogue, CD-ROM, the Internet or other electronic media. The virtual superstore exists now: it has a global clientèle and relies on companies like FedEx to get the product to the customer's door. This may be overnight for a premium or in six weeks for a discount – the point is that it arrives when the customer wants it, and it matches needs and demands. FedEx becomes a partner in creating the offer.

The acrimonious relationship between retailers and suppliers becomes redundant. Margins are higher for the producer, FedEx makes its margin and the customer gets a cheaper product delivered to his or her home. The intermediary is history.

Given the speed of change in international developments, competitiveness will increasingly rest on the benefit derived from these efficiencies. In this respect the old-fashioned view of a sequential approach to international marketing is redundant. In this scenario the company is global or dead. Whatever size the company may be, it will use international logistics to deliver global satisfactions. It can focus on tighter, more viable, niche markets, and will constantly refine these markets via database technology and the information generated about customers throughout the world. In the new marketing, the global players may be the equivalent of your local corner shop.

This new approach will require new thinking. Domestic logistics has traditionally relied on the experience of the firm and its logistics manager, if such a person exists. All of this becomes irrelevant in this scenario. The new global logistics manager needs to learn a new set of rules, requiring:

▓ anticipation of technical developments and changing customer requirements
▓ an understanding of currency impact on logistics
▓ expertise in cross-border shipping by whatever means
▓ understanding of international regulation and documentation
▓ a comprehensive knowledge of the transportation infrastructure
▓ benchmarking against global competitors
▓ understanding of IT systems and their role in logistics management
▓ understanding the benefit that customers require from logistics.

The task is serious – this is a highly strategic decision, and management must move now to create the new logistics for business in the next century.

The impact of global logistics

Logistics costs are falling dramatically. Lean production for global markets and 'fat' distribution are not feasible. Many companies are focusing on core competence, recognizing that concentrating on what they do best delivers both efficiency and value in terms of the product. However, customers may look for value beyond the functional product. The company may choose to add these values through partnership with logistics companies like Federal Express Business Logistics Services, whose core competence is logistics management.

FedEx will re-route products to its hubs around the world and deliver world-wide, guaranteeing two-day delivery.

Nike, for example, could state that its core business is design and marketing, not production and logistics; the value the customer seeks is configured by Nike through the partnerships it creates. These values can be extended infinitely – Nike could choose to create partnerships with providers of fitness programmes, with nutritionists, etc., combining diverse core competencies to create satisfactions to their customers needs.

Core values as defined today may not deliver the satisfactions demanded by customers. Partnerships and affinity marketing are a vision of the future of management of customer satisfactions.

GLOBAL INFRASTRUCTURE DEVELOPMENTS

The leading edge practitioners are developing around a hub and spoke systems. Containerization – the breakthrough of the 1960s – has resulted in a massive reduction in the cost of all transport modes: sea, air, road and rail. Today, companies are focusing their activities around megacontainer ports serviced by the next generation of container vessels. These mega-ports have become the hubs around which companies build their business. Today, and increasingly in the future, super-container vessels will run between these major hubs, with smaller ships feeding into the hubs via a series of spokes. The hubs become the regional centres for production, packaging, intraregional shipping and the location of regional headquarters.

A good example of this is Singapore. The same pattern is occurring around key airports, and air transport is developing in a similar fashion. However the latest developments combine sea and air, getting the best out of both transport modes. While sea transport presents the lowest cost option, it is also the slowest. Manufacturers and their customers demand the lowest cost and also demand the fastest response. Maximizing efficiency and balancing the cost/ response equation is the responsibility of marketing.

For example, bulk textiles and finished clothing are shipped from China to Los Angeles by sea. They are then transferred by air to Europe via LAX, the key airport in Los Angeles. In the same way, bulk materials are shipped from India to Sri Lanka and the finished product forwarded to Singapore for further distribution. Singapore acts as the access hub for other destinations, including the UK. The product does not go from Sri Lanka to the UK – it is more efficient to go via Singapore.

Amsterdam Port and Schipol airport, Singapore Port and Changi airport, and Hong Kong Port and Chek Lap Kok airport are all examples of the latest integration of transport modes, providing simple one-stop solutions for global business.

It is important that countries wishing their economies to thrive should invest now; otherwise they will be relegated to a spoke position. It will take vision, commitment and investment to create the future. From the European perspective, this requires a global strategy. It appears that governments are incapable of envisioning this strategy.

Our intention is not to describe the benefits of each mode of transport here, but the growth in air freight is interesting. The following facts illustrate the massive increase in air freight.

- 40 per cent of all world trade, by value, goes by air.
- In 1994, 60 billion kilometric tonnes were transported by air; in 1985, just 40 billion kilometric tonnes were flown.
- Aircraft capacities have risen from 10 tonnes to 100 tonnes per aircraft, with a consequent reduction in costs.
- FedEx is now the world's sixth largest airline in terms of fleet size.
- Even major people carriers like BA have a substantial cargo fleet, and the next generation of planes will be hybrids, with substantial freight capacity.

Schipol is now the global hub for cut flowers, taking roses from Ecuador and sunflowers from France as well as tulips from Amsterdam. They are shipped by air to destinations world-wide. What this means is that the old correlation between distance to market and selling prices is changing or redundant. The driving force behind these changes is the customer. Service is the prerogative of the customer, who demands:

- superior products
- free extras

■ faster delivery
■ lowest price/better value.

The customer service level is a strategic decisions within the organization. Its most obvious or visible manifestation is in inventory levels, which impact most acutely on delivery cycles. Within the UK, the Body Shop demands weekly delivery within a two-hour window of opportunity. Failure to comply means strict sanctions and the removal of bonus payments. Whilst this might be viewed as extreme and difficult to replicate, it is becoming more commonplace. For example, the intercontinental delivery of live lobsters takes place daily from Canada to the rest of the world. The product is delivered to hundreds of restaurants overnight via partner intermediaries, and the product must arrive before 8:30 a.m.

Furthermore, a New York pizza parlour promises delivery to any major city in the world within 24 hours.

INTRA-COUNTRY DISTRIBUTION

The company needs to consider the following points.

Density of distribution channel

The key question is: where does the product need to be so that customers can buy it? If you are not there, customers will not seek you out. With electronic distribution, less is becoming more: we now have branchless banks, ticketless travel and brokerless insurance.

The possible points of access

Create opportunity for your customers to access you. Procter & Gamble set objectives for increasing the number of complaints received. Call centres, coupled with other means of data gathering, give access as well as information, which can help up-sell or develop new product offerings and manage the product experience more closely.

Envision what the market-place might look like in five years and start planning strategically in that direction. What will the role of the Internet be? How will digital TV impact the international market?

Today's methods of distribution are changing rapidly. Traditional channels must show benefit and value or they are in danger of elimination.

THE LENGTH OF THE CHANNEL

For many products, the traditional routes to market will remain, particularly in the following situations:

▪ where channels remain complex or state controlled
▪ where cultural values determine the nature of distribution.

Japan still operates via an extended channel, despite a high-tech environment with each level connected via *Keiretsu* arrangements. This makes distribution expensive, as each link in the chain extracts its margin.

Elsewhere, channel lengths are shrinking in response to pressures which are becoming global.

The key to success is relationship marketing: planning on a partnership basis with intermediaries and considering each market on its own merits.

SUMMARY

Distribution and logistics are at the cutting edge of creation of competitive advantage.

Firms must plan for the long term, envision the future, anticipate change, and apply it to business practice.

More thinking must be done about valuing the channels from the point of view of the customer rather than seeing them as supply-side access routes.

Dialogue and relationships are the key factors.

Logistics involves strategic management decisions, and thus, alongside the management of brand equity, becomes one of the key areas in marketing.

11

A Pro Forma for International Marketing

INTRODUCTION

This chapter takes the form of a questionnaire, which has been designed to provide a format for the development of international marketing activity. The answers to the questionnaire should help to focus your international activity, and when used in conjunction with data sources should enable an input to the marketing plan for international markets.

It is almost certain that the information you have will be incomplete. Chapter 3, on research, gives you some ideas about where and how to find data on international markets.

The questionnaire has been developed by the authors, in conjunction with the DTI, Xexco, Microsoft and Barclays Bank, to be of use and benefit to smaller firms making initial enquiries into the feasibility of international marketing. The scheme is currently being piloted by a number of organizations and is ultimately designed to work with intelligent Web browsers.

THE QUESTIONNAIRE

Your company

Company name:

Company address:

How many staff are employed?

What business are you in (from the customer's point of view)?

SIC code:

Products handled:

Do you have any existing overseas activity?

In which countries:

What was your turnover for the last three years?

What percentage was from exporting?

Do you use the following services for help in running your business?

> Chambers of Commerce
> DTI
> Business Link
> TECs
> Your bank
> Consultants
> Trade associations
> Others (please specify):

What services are available to facilitate your move into international markets?

Whether to market overseas

Where are you now? Before you start, you need to assess your company's strategic capability.

- ■ Objectives: what are the development objectives for your company and where does an international marketing strategy fit in?
- ■ Rationale for international marketing
  - Is international marketing part of a planned strategic approach to expansion?
  - Have you considered the impact of international expansion on your existing activities?
  - Is there a real reason for exporting?
  - Is international activity/exporting part of your long-term plan?
  - Is your home market saturated?
  - Do you face increasing competition?
  - Do you have excess capacity?
  - Do you wish to diversify geographically?
  - Are there organizational reasons?
  - Are there financial reasons?
  - Is there a real opportunity?
- ■ How committed do you wish to be to marketing overseas?
  - To what extent do you wish to be involved?
  - Do you wish simply to export surplus production?
  - Do you wish to become actively involved in export marketing?
  - Do you wish to develop new products for overseas markets?
- ■ Resources: what are the resources of your company?
  - Marketing skills and experience
    What experience do your staff have of managing international markets?
    What research skills do your staff have?
  - Money
    What is your financial situation?
    What were your turnover and profit last year?
    Can you afford to invest in exporting?
    What funds are available to you?
    Do you have the backing of your bank?
    Do you have access to sound financial advice?
  - Management and people: are you committed?
    Do you have a committed workforce?
    Do your staff have experience in the export business?
    Do you have sufficient staff to deal with a new initiative?
    Would you need to recruit?
    In which areas would recruitment be necessary?
    What language skills exist among your staff?
    Are you willing/able to provide your staff with additional

training where required to support this venture?
Do staff work well in a team?
- Methods
  Do you have the organizational capability to deal with international markets?
▪ Will you need an export department?
  - Will it be a built in export department?
  - Staff: who is going to talk to the overseas customers?
  - Do your staff have:
    language skills?
      knowledge of documentation?
      specific export expertise?
      capacity available for export marketing tasks?
  - Can you fund an export operation?
  - Will you need an overseas representative?
  - Are your own staff capable?
  - Are your agents/distributors of sufficient calibre?
▪ Where To?
  Selecting a market or markets – you must consider the macro data in the next section.
  - Which country or countries are you interested in?

General country information

▪ Economy
  Among other questions you should analyse the following.
  - What is the economic system of the country?
  - Levels of GDP/GNP.
  - Wealth distribution.
  - How much does the government spend?
  - What are the taxation levels in the country?
  - What is the employment rate?
  - What are the common patterns of employment?
  - What is the extent of trade union activity, and what is the state of labour relations?
  - Retail prices (retail price index).
  - Composition of consumer credit – who does the lending?
  - What is the level of debt of the country?
  - What are the principal industries of the country?
  - Currency.
  - Exchange rates.
  - Trade incentives and barriers.

- What incentives are provided for exporters by the UK government?
- Promotional activities.
- What UK policies encourage exporters?
■ Geography
You may need to assess the impact of geographical factors.
- What is the climate of the country?
- What are the implications of climatic conditions?
- Are there any natural hazards associated with the country?
- Are all areas accessible?
- What is the physical size of the country?
■ Social demographic information
- What is the population of the country?
- What is the age structure of the population?
- What is the ethnic structure of the population?
- What is the birth rate of the country?
- What is the life expectancy of the population?
- What is the infant mortality rate among the population?
- Are there any patterns of immigration and emigration?
- What is the growth rate of the country, in terms of population?
- Where do the people live?
- Changing consumption patterns – what do the people spend money on and how has this been developing over time?
- What is the main language of the country?
- What other languages are commonly spoken?
- What is the average size of households?
- How do people live in the country – what is the family structure?
- Who has an income – who spends the money, how much and on what?
- What is the literacy rate of the population?
- What proportion of the people are educated, and to what level?
- What is the religion of the country, and what are the implications of this (working days, attitude to women, clothing, food, religious festivals, provisions for prayer)?
■ Political
You should consider the following points.
- Political stability.
- Political system. What is the type or form of government organization in the country (monarchy, republic, dictatorship and so on)?
- The number and nature of political parties.

- The role of local or regional government.
- International organization and treaty obligations.
- Power or economic bloc grouping.
- Membership of formal and informal political, military and economic blocs, and the explicit and implicit obligations of such blocs.
- Are there political beliefs in the country, not a formal part of government philosophy, which may affect behaviour – for example Nationalism?
- How are political relations between the UK and the country and the country and the rest of the world?

■ Ethical/environmental
- Are there any ethical concerns associated with the country in terms of, for example, human rights violations or excessive environmental degradation?
- Also consider this in terms of your product – is it exploitative? Would it offend the values of the country?
- What is the impact on home market activity?
- What environmental standards are in place?
- How much will you need to adapt the product and the rest of the marketing mix?

■ Technical
  What is the standard of the infrastructure in terms of the following.
- distribution, including road, rail, air and sea transport links
- public transport provision
- power and energy
- water provision
- communications
- IT

■ Legal information
- What is the legal system of the country (code law or common law)?
- What are the legal constraints within the country?
- Contract law.
- Employment law.
- Relevant legal rules for foreign business.
- Discriminatory labour and tax legislation and so on, applied only to foreign-owned firms.
- Import–export restrictions.
- International investment restrictions.
- Profit repatriation restrictions.
- Exchange control restrictions.

- Membership of and obligations to international financial organizations.
- Government regulations.
- License requirements.
- Prohibitions.
- Qualitative controls.
- Regulations on market entry.
- Currency exchange controls.
- Health and safety legislation.
- Technical and quality standards.
- Environment legislation.
- Commercial legal environment.
- Barriers to trade.
- Quotas.
- Tariffs.
- Voluntary quotas.
- Countervailing duties.

■ Competitors
- Who are your competitors? Who manufactures and sells similar products – both within the country and through exporting?
- What other UK firms export to this country?
- What other companies are involved?
- What is the structure of the competition – number and types of competitors?
- What are the strengths of your competitors?
- What are the weaknesses of your competitors?
- In what way is the competition you face influenced by general business, cultural, economic and social conditions?
- Costs.
- Laws and regulations relating to the competitive environment?
- What makes your competitors successful?
- Do they have a unique product?
- Price?
- Good brand/reputation?
- Control of distribution channels?
- Relationships with key customers?
- Technological advantage?
- Management skills?
- Service levels?
- What makes you better than them?
- How do you monitor competition in international markets?

▪ Customer characteristics and culture
What are the implications for your export plans in terms of local culture? Consider the following points.
  – Religion?
  – Design and aesthetics?
  – Language?
  – Levels of education?
  – Attitudes and values?
  – Social structures?
  – Diversity of cultural groupings.
  – What cultural groupings exist and what are the principal differences between the groupings?
  – Nature of decision making.
  – How are deals made?
  – Do cultural differences arise in techniques of negotiating, for example bartering?
  – Are business deals based around connections, family ties or similar?
  – Can deals be made quickly?
  – Who makes the decisions – can you identify these people?
  – What are the major influences on purchasing behaviour?
▪ The market
  – Can you establish market size in volume and value over time?
  – How is the market forecast to grow?
  – What is the basic market structure?
  – Of the people who buy the product, how often do they buy, in what quantity, and for what purpose?
  – Can you establish market share in volume and value over time?
  – Do potential customers need to buy your product or could they purchase an alternative product
▪ Can your customers pay you?
  – What price can you charge?
  – How much do your competitors charge?
  – What margins do your intermediaries require?
  – Can you compete on this basis?
  – Terms and conditions of payment.
  – What about insurance?
▪ Currency
  – How stable is the currency of the country to which you wish to export?
  – How has the currency fluctuated over time?

- How does the currency compare with Sterling?
- Can you manage exposure to risk in this area?
- Exchange control restrictions.
- What are the formal legal and administrative controls on the conversion of the local currency to any or all foreign currencies?

■ Channels
- How does the product get to the end user?
- Capabilities of intermediaries.
- Are they available?
- What is their quality?
- What experience do they have?
- In which markets?
- Which products do they have experience in handling?
- Can they help with marketing research?
- What is the size of the company?
- What experience does the company have with your product line?
- How is its sales force organized, and what is the quality of the sales force?
- Could the company provide after sales-service, if required, and what would be the quality of this service?
- What experience and knowledge do they have of promotion techniques?
- Do they have a good reputation with customers?
- How strong are they financially? Do they have a good credit rating?
- Do they enjoy good relations with local government?
- What languages are spoken within the company?
- How willing will they be to cooperate with your company?
- Legal considerations – how will the contracts be drawn up?

■ Communication
- Promotion – can you promote your product locally?
- What do your competitors do?
- Will you need to adapt your current promotions?
- Which media are available?
- How much will it cost?
- Are there laws controlling promotions?
- Can you effectively evaluate the success of your promotions?
- Can you produce publicity materials in the local market?
- Who will you be represented by in the country?
- Will you need a local sales force?

▓ What to sell
  – Do you need to change your product to suit local conditions?
  – Are modifications to the product required, in terms of:
      The product itself?
      Local demand?
      Local standards – legal implications?
      Local materials?
      Cultural requirements?
      Technical specifications?
      Packaging?
      Design?
      Language?
      Legal requirements?
      Branding?
      Product and company name?
      Selling platform, strapline?
      Image in relation to your competitors?

Contingencies

Do you have a fully costed and researched exit strategy?

12

World Trade Infrastructure

INTRODUCTION

To get your international marketing into action you will need to research one or a number of markets, and to put that research into context you will need at least an overview of the state of world trade at the time that this book was written.

Much of the data used below to illustrate the world trade infrastructure will, by the time you read it, be out of date. Indeed, it is in the nature of trade statistics that they are invariably produced after the fact and with considerable compromises on the way – as we shall see below, some forms of trade are hardly reported at all.

Furthermore the pace of change in world trading conditions is rapid and, in a period of uncertainty in almost all economies around the world, seems to be becoming more complex.

In this chapter we look at the overall size and scope of global trade and how the major regions of the world interact. A comparison of the world's major economies with those just beginning to make their presence felt on the global stage gives a basis for comparing market opportunities and the sources of potential threats in the broadest sense.

We also look slightly beyond the usual macro measures of economies to look at the increasing importance of service industries – trade that is, if not always invisible, certainly difficult to measure. Finally, we look at what is, perhaps, the most significant driver of trade going into the new millennium – communications and technology.

THE BIG PICTURE

According to the World Trade Organisation (WTO), world cross-border trade is estimated to have surpassed $6,000 billion for the first time in 1995. In that year trade grew by around 8 per cent (in volume) – somewhat less than in 1994, but nevertheless better than the average for the preceding five years. In 1996, however, growth seemed to have slowed as a result of reduced consumer demand in Europe and North America. The 5 per cent expected for the full-year figures for 1996 is still considered by many to be a reasonable and sustainable rate of growth – as good as 1990 and better than four out of the previous 10 years.

Crucially, in 1995, that 8 per cent increase in trade was larger than the 3 per cent increase in world merchandize output, also estimated by the WTO. For developing countries (not including those which are oil exporters) the ratio of trade to Gross Domestic Product (GDP) in 1995 was 30 per cent; in 1970 it was 10 per cent. In other words, goods and services – for all economies – are increasingly being traded across borders. Globalization is a reality.

The United Nations Conference on Trade and Development (UNCTAD) figures (Table 12.1) paint a picture of the world's economies in their varying states of development and their relative contribution to the world economy over the last few years for which figures are available.

Growth overall proves to have been greater in the developing or transitional economies. Because of their lower base, however, they had relatively little impact on the global figure. However, the contrast between a high of +2.8 per cent change in the output of the most developed nations and the most recent figure of +4.5 per cent for the developing economies is significant.

To see how the regions of the world interact – how they trade – the figures from the WTO for merchandise are revealing (Table 12.2). Rather than focus on notions of relative development, the WTO figures refer to the increasing importance of regional trading blocks.

Similar patterns emerge for agriculture, mining and manufactures (Tables 12.3–12.5): a concentration of share within regions but, significantly, Asia second only in importance to Western Europe.

The regions of the world are, of course dominated to a greater or lesser extent by key countries within them – North America is, essentially, the USA, and Asia's performance is, if not dominated, then at least spearheaded by Japan. Within Europe the strongest economies have been Germany, France, Italy and the UK.

Table 12.1 *World output, 1991–96*
(percentage increase based on 1990 dollars)

Region/country	1991	1992	1993	1994	1995*	1996*
World	0.6	1.4	1.1	2.8	2.4	2.4
Developed market-economy						
countries	0.9	1.6	0.7	2.8	2.0	1.9
of which						
USA	−1.0	2.7	2.2	3.5	2.0	2.2
Japan	4.0	1.1	0.1	0.5	0.9	2.1
European Union	1.5	1.0	−0.6	2.8	2.5	1.3
of which						
Germany	5.0	2.2	−1.2	2.9	1.9	0.5
France	0.8	1.2	−1.3	2.8	2.2	0.9
Italy	1.2	0.7	−1.2	2.2	3.0	1.5
United Kingdom	−2.0	−0.5	2.3	3.8	2.4	2.2
C/E Europe/Baltic States/CIS	−11.7	−13.4	−8.3	−10.1	−2.6	0.3
Developing countries	2.9	3.6	3.7	4.7	4.0	4.5
of which						
America	3.5	2.5	3.4	4.9	0.7	2.4
Africa	1.9	0.7	0.1	2.6	2.8	3.1
Asia	2.8	5.0	4.6	5.1	6.3	6.1
China	8.4	14.3	14.0	11.8	10.2	9.0

*Figures for 1995 and 1996 are estimates and forecasts respectively.
Source: *Trade and Development Report 1996*. UNCTAD.

THE BIG PLAYERS

The apparent dominance of the USA, Europe and Japan has led to the concept of the 'triad' of economies first outlined by Kenichi Ohmae (1989). Tables 12.6 gives a profile of the prime movers in global trade. However, these figures bear comparison with those for other, developing economies.

RISING STARS

As the figures on global trade intimated, the major developed economies remain powerful. But their positions are not unchallenged (Table 12.7).

The top 50 merchandise exporters in 1996 included Argentina, Chile, Finland, Mexico, Poland, South Korea, Sweden and the

Table 12.2 *Percentage share of intra- and inter-regional trade flows in world merchandise exports, 1995*

Destination Origin	North America	Latin America	Western Europe	C/E Europe/ Baltic/CIS	Africa	Middle East	Asia	World
North America	5.7	2.0	3.0	0.1	0.2	0.4	4.3	15.9
Latin America	2.2	1.0	0.8	0.0	0.1	0.0	0.5	4.6
Western Europe	3.3	1.1	30.9	2.0	1.2	1.2	4.3	44.8
C/E Europe/Baltic States/CIS	0.2	0.1	1.8	0.6	0.0	0.1	0.4	3.1
Africa	0.3	0.0	1.1	0.0	0.2	0.0	0.3	2.1
Middle East	0.3	0.1	0.7	0.0	0.1	0.2	1.4	2.9
Asia	6.3	0.6	4.4	0.3	0.4	0.6	13.5	26.6
World	18.4	4.8	42.7	3.1	2.3	2.6	24.7	100.0

Note: Total value of world merchandise trade = $4890 billion.
Source: *World Trade Organisation Annual Report 1996.* WTO.

Table 12.3 Percentage share of intra- and inter-regional trade flows in world exports of agricultural products, 1995

Destination Origin	North America	Latin America	Western Europe	C/E Europe/ Baltic/CIS	Africa	Middle East	Asia	World
North America	4.5	1.9	3.4	0.3	0.7	0.6	8.0	19.4
Latin America	2.5	1.9	3.5	0.2	0.4	0.3	1.6	10.3
Western Europe	1.7	0.8	32.8	2.3	1.6	1.1	2.6	42.2
C/E Europe/Baltic States/CIS	0.1	0.1	1.9	0.8	0.1	0.1	0.6	3.7
Africa	0.2	0.0	2.1	0.1	0.5	0.1	0.6	3.5
Middle East	0.0	0.0	0.4	0.0	0.1	0.4	0.1	1.0
Asia	1.8	0.2	2.7	0.3	0.4	0.7	12.0	18.9
World	10.8	5.0	46.7	4.1	3.6	3.2	25.5	100.0

Note: Total value of world agricultural trade = $579 billion.
Source: *World Trade Organisation Annual Report 1996*. WTO.

Table 12.4 *Percentage share of intra- and inter-regional trade flows in world exports of mining products, 1995*

Destination Origin	North America	Latin America	Western Europe	C/E Europe/ Baltic/CIS	Africa	Middle East	Asia	World
North America	5.6	1.0	1.7	0.0	0.1	0.1	2.2	10.8
Latin America	4.4	2.2	1.6	0.1	0.1	0.0	1.4	9.9
Western Europe	2.0	0.3	20.7	0.6	0.4	0.4	1.1	26.0
C/E Europe/Baltic States/CIS	0.5	0.0	5.5	2.0	0.0	0.0	0.8	8.9
Africa	2.2	0.2	4.6	0.1	0.6	0.1	1.1	8.9
Middle East	1.9	0.5	4.0	0.1	0.6	0.8	11.3	19.9
Asia	0.8	0.1	0.9	0.1	0.0	0.1	13.0	15.7
World	17.4	4.3	38.9	3.0	1.9	1.5	30.9	100.0

Note: Total value of world mining trade = $512 billion.
Source: *World Trade Organisation Annual Report 1996.* WTO.

Table 12.5 *Percentage share of intra- and inter-regional trade flows in world exports of manufactures, 1995*

Destination	North America	Latin America	Western Europe	C/E Europe/ Baltic/CIS	Africa	Middle East	Asia	World
Origin								
North America	5.8	2.2	3.0	0.1	0.2	0.3	4.0	15.7
Latin America	1.9	0.7	0.3	0.0	0.0	0.0	0.2	3.1
Western Europe	3.8	1.3	31.9	2.2	1.3	1.3	5.1	47.5
C/E Europe/Baltic States/CIS	0.1	0.1	1.3	0.4	0.0	0.1	0.3	2.3
Africa	0.1	0.0	0.5	0.0	0.1	0.0	0.1	0.8
Middle East	0.2	0.0	0.3	0.0	0.0	0.1	0.2	0.9
Asia	8.0	0.7	5.2	0.3	0.4	0.7	14.0	29.8
World	19.9	5.0	42.4	3.0	2.1	2.6	24.0	100.0

Note: Total value of world manufactures trade = $3640 billion.
Source: *World Trade Organisation Annual Report 1996*. WTO.

Table **12.6** *Some key dimensions of major economies*

	GDP (PPP) ($billion)	GDP real growth (%)	GDP per capita ($)	GDP composition (%) Agriculture	Industry	Services	Population (millions)	Population growth rate (%)
USA	7,247	2.1	27,500	2	23	75	266	0.91
Japan	2,679	0.3	21,300	2	40	58	125	0.21
Europe								
Germany	1,452	1.8	17,900	1	34	65	84	0.67
France	117	2.4	20,200	2	26	71	58	0.34
Italy	1,088	3.2	18,700	3	32	66	57	0.13
United Kingdom	1,138	2.7	19,500	2	28	71	58	0.22

Source: *World Factbook 1996*. CIA.

Table 12.7 Some key dimensions of 'rising star' economies

	GDP (PPP) ($billion)	GDP real growth (%)	GDP per capita ($)	GDP composition (%) Agriculture	Industry	Services	Population (millions)	Population growth rate (%)
China	3,500	10.3	2,900	19	48	33	1210	0.98
Hong Kong	152	5.0	27,500	<1	18	81	6	1.77
India	1,408	5.5	1,500	N/A	N/A	N/A	952	1.64
Malaysia	194	9.5	9,800	8	25	67	19	2.07
Philippines	180	4.8	2,530	22	30	48	74	2.18
Singapore	66	8.9	22,900	–	28	72	3	1.90
South Korea	591	9.0	13,000	8	45	47	45	1.02
Taiwan	290	6.0	13,510	4	37	59	21	0.89
Thailand	417	8.6	6,900	10	31	59	59	1.07

NB World Bank estimate of China's GDP may overestimate by as much as 25 per cent
Source: *World Factbook 1996*. CIA.

Philippines, each of which experienced growth in the value of their exports of more than 30 per cent. Similarly, Brazil, Chile, the Czech Republic, Malaysia, Poland, South Korea, South Africa, Thailand, Turkey and Venezuela all saw merchandise imports rise in value by more than 30 per cent.

It is becoming increasingly apparent that the Asian 'leg' of the triad is more than just Japan, and that intra-regional trade is becoming as significant as inter-regional trade. Again, according to the WTO, the intra-regional exports of the developing Asian economies (totaling $287 billion in 1995) were approaching those of North America and Western Europe, which combined were $314 billion.

As consumers too, the developing Asian economies represented an increasingly important market for Europe and North America.

Although the success of the so-called 'tiger' economies has been well reported, it is worth giving some comparisons of their industrial strength.

The production and consumption of steel and energy can often give an indication of the strength of industry in an economy. Globally, in 1994, steel consumption was stabilizing at 622 million tonnes, and among OECD countries – predominantly the most developed – it had declined for the preceding three years before increasing by 8 per cent from 1993 to 1994. In Japan in particular the decline continued.

In stark contrast to these figures – taken as indicative of the world recession – steel consumption in South Korea rose by 20 per cent. In China a fall of 10.7 per cent in 1994 was on a consumption figure which, in the previous year, had leapt up by almost 40 per cent!

The OECD predicted at that point that, amid a general rise in consumption, trade and production, China's production of crude steel would approach 100 million tonnes – roughly equal to that of Japan.

Perhaps the most surprising figures are those which describe the sheer scale of the Chinese economy. The largest producer of coal in the world, China produces more than 25 per cent of the world's coal and ranks highly in the world's producers of electricity. However, with its huge population China's consumption of power per capita (Table 12.8) is comparatively tiny.

China's size throws up some other surprising comparisons (eg Table 12.9) – indicators of its influence, or potential influence, on the world.

Table 12.8 *Electricity capacity and consumption per capita*

North America	Europe	Asia	Kilowatt hours	Consumption per capita
USA			695,120,000	11,236
		Japan	205,140,000	6,262
		China	162,000,000	593
	Germany		115,430,000	5,683
Canada			108,090,000	16,133
	France		105,250,000	6,149
		India	81,200,000	324
	UK		65,360,000	5,123
	Italy		61,630,000	4,033
	Spain		43,800,000	3,545
	Sweden		34,560,000	14,891
	Poland		31,120,000	2,908
	Norway		27,280,000	23,735
		South Korea	26,940,000	2,847
	Romania		22,180,000	2,076
		Taiwan	21,460,000	4,789

Source: *Gale Country & World Rankings Reporter*, 2nd edn (data from *CIA World Factbook*, 1995).

Table 12.9 *Engineering graduates produced in 1995*

Country	Number of graduates
China	113,000
Japan	81,000
USA	80,000
Germany	38,000
Mexico	30,000
India	29,000
South Korea	28,000
Czech Republic	9,400
Taiwan	8,900

Source: *Gale Country & World Rankings Reporter*, 2nd edn.

Clearly, despite China's relatively low standards of living its size and the resources applied to education have had a considerable effect. In 1994, according to the UN, China earned almost $3 billion from the export of engineering and construction services – only just over 3 per cent of the revenue of the top 225 firms, but nevertheless a creditable share compared with the US at 16 per cent or Germany with 11 per cent. Notable also is the inclusion in Table 12.9 of nations such as South Korea and India. South Korea earned slightly more than China from its export of engineering skills. India, in particular, has begun to carve out a niche for itself in the global market as a supplier of highly trained but comparatively low-wage workers. The example of BA's ticketing services being carried out in India is well known.

It is interesting to see how some of this educational capital is being built (Table 12.10). The USA is one of the most popular destinations for Asian students studying abroad.

Table 12.10 *Number of Asian students studying in the USA, 1996*

Country of origin	Number of students
China	82,000
Japan	43,800
India	34,800
South Korea	31,100
Hong Kong	13,800
Malaysia	13,700
Indonesia	11,700
Thailand	9,500
Singapore	5,400

Source: *Gale Country & World Rankings Reporter*, 2nd Edition.

China's position within the world has, of course, changed very recently. With the handover of Hong Kong to Chinese rule, China is now better placed than ever before to enter the world economy, both as a major supplier and as a market. A startling example is the huge market that China represents for the entertainment business: it is the largest cinema audience in the world, with 5 billion tickets estimated to have been sold in 1995 and some 160 million households with television sets.

The ability of an emerging economy to begin to compete in the provision of global services should not be underestimated. Where communications allow, services can, in effect, be delivered remotely rather than face-to-face, and the cost of the labour element of a service can be crucial.

Where face-to-face dealing is required, the volume of air traffic between the continents of the world gives an idea of the ease with which this need is met (Tables 12.11 and 12.12).

Figures for the top ten airports by three measures are given in Table 12.13.

The USA dominates the air transport world, being the wealthiest nation in a pivotal position for international trade. Hong Kong, Singapore and Bangkok enjoy similar positions and have almost no strictly 'domestic' traffic.

Other forms of communication are dealt with below.

SERVICE INCLUDED?

Another look at the comparative 'key indicator' tables above (Tables 12.6 and 12.7) shows the importance of the service sector, both to the most developed economies and to many of the developing ones. Increasingly, there seems to be almost no product which does not have an element of service embodied in or associated with it. In 1970, according to the recent World Economic and Social Survey from the UN, services accounted for 55 per cent of the combined GDP of developed and developing economies, while 20 years later it accounted for 65 per cent.

In the UN report it was noted that business services in particular are difficult to quantify in world trade. Not only are communications, financial services, software, computer services, royalties, construction and engineering, advertising and many other forms of service supplied by foreign-owned companies in other countries, but they are increasingly traded across frontiers and supplied globally.

The most recent UN figures for global trade in *all* services are for 1994, when they estimate that the value was equivalent to around 22 per cent of the value of merchandise trade. In fact, they report this proportion as having been relatively static for the last 25 years. This is explained in part by the driving down of costs in two major segments of the services sector: transport and travel. By contrast business services have become increasingly valuable. In 1994 the export of these services totaled $410 billion.

As you would expect, the most developed economies dominate the provision of business services that are exported. Likewise, they are the greatest importers. In rank order the seven top suppliers in

Table 12.11 Major air traffic flows of passengers between regions, *1995* (percentage of IATA scheduled international passengers)

	North America	Central America	South America	Europe	Africa	Middle East	Asia	South-west Pacific
North America	2.3	5.4	2.0	10.4	–	–	5.3	1.4
Central America		–	–	–	–	–	–	–
South America			0.5	–	–	–	–	–
Europe				37.9	3.5	1.9	5.5	–
Africa					1.1	1.0	–	–
Middle East						0.7	2.1	–
Asia							12.2	2.9
South-west Pacific								0.6

Note: Total scheduled international passengers 273,012,000. Figures represented by '–' less than 1 per cent.
Source: *World Air Transport Statistics.* IATA 1996.

Table 12.12 *Major air traffic flows of freight between regions, 1995 (percentage of IATA scheduled international traffic – freight tonnes)*

	North America	Central America	South America	Europe	Africa	Middle East	Asia	South-west Pacific
North America	0.6	1.1	1.7	18.8	–	–	11.7	–
Central America		–	–	1.1	–	–	–	–
South America			0.3	1.3	–	–	–	–
Europe				11.4	4.3	3.8	14.6	–
Africa					0.8	–	–	–
Middle East						0.4	1.8	–
Asia							17.5	3.5
South-west Pacific								0.9

Note: Total scheduled international passengers 273,012,000. Figures represented by '–' less than 1 per cent.
Source: *World Air Transport Statistics*. IATA 1996.

Table 12.13 *The top 10 airports: passengers and freight*

Airport	Passengers – terminal*	Airport	International passengers handled	Airport	Cargo (tonnes)
Chicago	67,254,586	London Heathrow	46,806,090	Tokyo	1,662,852
Atlanta	57,322,670	Frankfurt	30,256,700	Los Angeles	1,597,219
Dallas/Ft Worth	54,298,930	Hong Kong	27,423,656	Miami	1,584,680
London Heathrow	54,107,152	Paris	25,533,719	New York	1,572,840
Los Angeles	53,909,223	Amsterdam	24,709,096	Hong Kong	1,484,741
Tokyo	45,779,184	Singapore	21,743,196	Frankfurt	1,461,284
Frankfurt	37,477,393	Tokyo	21,487,798	Chicago	1,235,806
San Francisco	36,260,064	London Gatwick	20,600,431	Seoul	1,215,968
Miami	33,235,658	New York	16,672,506	London Heathrow	1,125,608
Denver	31,028,191	Bangkok	15,119,065	Singapore	1,124,835

*Terminal passengers = sum of terminating passengers and transfer passengers (who are counted both on arrival and on departure.

Source: *World Air Transport Statistics*. IATA 1996.

1994 were the USA, the Netherlands, France, Japan, the UK, Germany and Italy, together accounting for two thirds of business service exports. Of these, only Japan, Germany and Italy were in deficit in terms of the balance of business services trade.

Of the top 30 countries in business services there were five Asian nations: Singapore, the Philippines, South Korea, Malaysia and Thailand. Singapore was the only significant net exporter. Is this then an opportunity for Western industry to enter Asian markets?

The WTO, in their annual report, gave figures for the export and import of commercial services by regions (Tables 12.14 and 12.15). They show how, in fact, developing economies and Asia are making the biggest strides forward in servicing the world.

COMMUNICATIONS

The same UN report quoted above with regard to business services pointed out that the most dynamic area of growth was in information-related services – telecoms, software development, and computer and data services. Globally, expenditures for 1995 were estimated at $325 billion.

The increasing ease with which services can be supplied at a distance from the consumer has already been stated and it is clear that telecommunications, and particularly the development of the Internet, are significant drivers.

The pace of change in communications technology is astonishing. It is only since the 1970s that most developed nations have had automatic switching for trunk calls. Without this technology, it is estimated that in any given city half the populations would have to be employed manually connecting calls to maintain the current volume of traffic.

Telecoms companies have become among the most global and the most profitable (Table 12.16).

However, traditional telecommunications companies may not have the future all to themselves. Stewart Brand, the controversial 'futurologist' and co-founder of the Global Business Network, foresees the arrival in just a few years of a truly global network of low-level satellites giving everyone rapid access to the Internet. Such a system – the Teledesic Network – is proposed by Microsoft and McCaw and will use 840 satellites around the globe.

Problems still remain to be solved, in particular the question of bandwidth – the volume of data which can be carried down any

Table 12.14 World exports of commercial services by selected region, 1985–94 (billion dollars and percentage)

Region	Value 1994	Share 1995	Share 1990	Share 1994	Annual percentage change 1990–94	Annual percentage change 1992	Annual percentage change 1993	Annual percentage change 1994
World	1,035	100.0	100.0	100.0	7	13	0	9
North America	197	19.0	19.1	19.0	7	8	1	7
USA	178	16.7	17.3	17.2	7	9	1	7
Latin America	39	4.7	3.7	3.8	8	10	5	10
Mexico	9	1.2	0.9	0.8	5	3	2	5
Brazil	5	0.5	0.5	0.5	7	22	-2	23
Western Europe	509	50.8	53.7	49.1	5	14	-5	8
European Union	457	44.9	47.8	44.1	5	14	-6	8
Africa	22	3.0	2.4	2.2	5	14	1	2
Egypt	8	0.8	0.6	0.7	12	15	0	9
South Africa	4	0.5	0.4	0.4	2	4	-2	11
Asia	220	16.1	16.7	21.2	13	13	13	17
Japan	57	5.4	5.2	5.5	8	10	8	10

Source: World Trade Organisation Annual Report 1996. WTO.

Table 12.15 *World imports of commercial services by selected region, 1985–94 (billion dollars and percentage)*

Region	Value 1994	Share 1995	Share 1990	Share 1994	Annual percentage change 1990-94	1992	1993	1994
World	1,045	100.0	100.0	100.0	6	13	1	8
North America	153	17.3	14.8	14.6	6	8	7	8
USA	125	14.2	11.9	11.9	6	5	9	10
Latin America	49	5.5	4.2	4.7	9	12	10	8
Mexico	13	1.3	1.2	1.2	6	9	1	8
Brazil	10	0.8	0.8	0.9	10	4	39	7
Western Europe	479	41.1	48.8	45.7	4	16	-6	7
European Union	444	36.8	43.7	42.4	5	17	-6	7
Africa	32	5.2	3.3	3.0	4	9	3	3
Egypt	5	0.7	0.4	0.5	13	55	11	4
South Africa	5	0.6	0.5	0.5	7	15	5	7
Asia	266	20.3	22.1	25.4	10	13	8	14
Japan	105	8.6	10.6	10.1	5	7	3	10

Source: *World Trade Organisation Annual Report 1996*. WTO.

Table 12.16 *The top 20 telecoms carriers in the world, 1995*

Rank position	Company	Nationality	Sales of computers ($bn)
1	NTT	Japan	61.5
2	AT&T	USA	47.3
3	Deutsche Telekom	Germany	44.4
4	France Telecom	France	29.6
5	BT	UK	22.1
6	GTE	USA	20.0
7	Telecom Italia	Italy	18.5
8	BellSouth	USA	17.9
9	MCI Communications	USA	15.3
10	Ameritech	USA	13.7
11	Nynex	USA	13.4
12	Bell Atlantic	USA	12.8
13	Sprint	USA	12.8
14	SBC Communications	USA	12.7
15	US West	USA	11.7
16	Telefonica	Spain	10.8
17	Telestra	Australia	10.4
18	Korea Telecom	South Korea	9.7
19	Telmex	Mexico	9.6
20	Telebras	Brazil	9.4

Source: *Telecommunications. A profile of the worldwide telecommunications industry.* 4th edn. Reed Electronic Research, 1997.

particular part of a network. The Teledesic Network is criticized for lacking bandwidth, which has a negative impact on speed of access.

For terrestrial networks the problem may be solved by the development of existing optic fibre networks. However, these may be monopolized by major telecom suppliers and are limited. In the USA, for example, there are 12 million miles of optic fibre, compared with 1.2 billion miles of standard copper wire. Most of the copper wire is in local neighbourhoods and places a limitation on the volume and speed of data delivery – the 'final mile' problem.

For every 100 inhabitants in the USA there are just over 57 main telephone lines, a number exceeded only by Canada (60), Sweden (68) and Switzerland (62), but being approached by most Western European countries with more than 40 and others such as Taiwan (39), Hong Kong (50), Japan (48), South Korea (38) and Singapore (40). In countries such as India and China, penetration of telephone lines is only one or two per hundred population.

The Internet is nevertheless a powerful competitive force, driven by the increasing affordability and penetration of computing capability. Since 1987 the average price of 1 Mbyte of hard disk storage capacity has fallen from around $13 to less than $1, and the the sales of hard disk storage have multiplied more than a hundredfold. Again the most developed countries lead the way. The top 10 computer companies for 1996 are shown in Table 12.17.

Table 12.17 *The top 10 computer companies in the world, 1996*

Rank position	Company	Nationality	Sales ($bn)
1	IBM	USA	75.9
2	Hewlett-Packard	USA	31.4
3	Fujitsu	Japan	29.7
4	Compaq	USA	18.1
5	Hitachi	Japan	15.2
6	NEC	Japan	15.1
7	Electronic Data Systems	USA	14.4
8	Toshiba	Japan	14.0
9	Digital Equipment Corporation	USA	13.7
10	Microsoft	USA	9.4

Source: *Datamation* quoted in the *Guardian*, 3 July 1997.

In 1986 the top 10 were IBM, Unisys, DEC, Fujitsu, NEC, Hitachi, Hewlett-Packard, Siemens (Germany), NCR and Olivetti (Italy). Microsoft at that time was in 96th position!

The use of the Internet is difficult to estimate. The figures in Table 12.18 give an indication of the penetration into the economies shown.

What is remarkable is the pattern of growth with penetration at least doubling in all the countries listed. Singapore, while at one time seeking to resist the effects of the Internet revolution, has now begun to position itself as a would-be major player in cyberspace.

The market for information technology is expanding at a greater rate for developing countries than for developed countries. Within the OECD, IT spending is estimated to have grown *annually* by 7.8 per cent between 1987 and 1994. For the same period the IT market expanded by 17.9 per cent per year for South Korea, over 18 per cent for Singapore and Hong Kong and 17 per cent for China. South American economies showed even greater growth: by 11.4 per cent for Brazil – approaching $5 billion – and over 34 per cent for Argentina, 29 per cent for Chile and 20 per cent for Colombia, although these three are from a much smaller base.

Table 12.18 *Internet hosts 1995 and 1996*

Country	Hosts per 1000	Hosts per 1000*
Iceland	18	42
Finland	14	62
USA	13	31
Norway	12	30
Australia	9	24
New Zealand	9	23
Sweden	9	23
Singapore	n/a	18
Switzerland	7	18
Canada	7	23
Netherlands	6	16
Denmark	5	15
UK	4	11
Austria	4	10

Source: *Information Technology Outlook 1995*, OECD, and *Gale Country and World Rankings*, 2nd edn, 1997.

Since 1987, the OECD estimates that spending on software particularly has grown annually by 12.3 per cent – double the growth rate of GDP member countries and two and a half times spending on hardware.

Perhaps the most telling figures are those estimates for the number of users – the global web community. The number of email accounts for 1995 were estimated to be 30 million and web users 10 million. By 2000 these figures are forecast to be 300 million and 200 million respectively.

Sources

1997 Telecommunications. A profile of the worldwide telecommunications industry — market prospects to 1999, 4th edn. Reed Electronic Research, 1997.

Directory of Trade Statistics. International Monetary Fund, 1996.

Gale Country & World Rankings Reporter, 2nd edn (ed. Brigitte T. Dornay). Gale Research, 1997.

Information Technology Outlook. Organization for Economic Co-operation and Development, 1995.

The Economist, 7 December 1996.

The Guardian, 3 July 1997.

The Steel Market in 1994 and the Outlook for 1995 and 1996. Organization for Economic Co-operation and Development, 1995.

The World Factbook, 1996. Central Intelligence Agency, 1996.

Trade and Development Report, 1996. United Nations Conference on Trade and Development, 1996.

World Economic and Social Survey 1996. United Nations, 1996.

World Market Share Reporter 1996 (ed. Robert Shazich). Gale Research, 1996.

WTO Annual Report, 1996, Volumes I and II. World Trade Organisation, 1996.

Further Reading

Albaum, G S *et al* (1994) *International Marketing and Export Management*, 2nd edn, Addison-Wesley, Reading MA.

Bradley, F (1995) *International Marketing Strategy*, 2nd edn, Prentice Hall, Englewood Cliffs NJ.

Buzzell, R D, Quelch, J A and Bartlett, C A (1995) *Global Marketing Management: Cases and Readings*, 3rd edn, Addison-Wesley, Reading MA.

Czinkota, M R and Ronkainen, I A (1995) *Readings in Global Marketing*, Dryden, Fort Worth TX.

Czinkota, M R and Ronkainen, I A (1996) *Global Marketing*, International Edition, Dryden, Fort Worth TX.

Douglas, S P and Craig, C S (1995) *Global Marketing Strategy*, McGraw-Hill, London.

Fifield, P and Lewis, K (1997) International Marketing Strategy, 2nd edn, Butterworth-Heinemann, Oxford.

Jain, S C (1996) *International Marketing Management*, 5th edn, Wadsworth, Belmont CA.

Jeannet, J-P and Hennessey, H D (1995) *Global Marketing Strategies*, 3rd edn, Houghton Mifflin, New York.

Keegan, W J (1995) *Global Marketing Management*, 5th edn, Prentice Hall, Englewood Cliffs NJ.

Majaro, S (1993) *International Marketing*, Routledge, London.

Onkvisit, S and Shaw, J J (1997) *International Marketing*, 3rd edn, Prentice Hall, Englewood Cliffs NJ.

Phillips, C, Doole, I and Lowe, R (1994) *International Marketing Strategy*, Routledge, London.

Terpstra, V and Sarathy, R (1997) *International Marketing*, 7th edn, Dryden, Fort Worth TX.

Usunier, J C (1996) *Marketing Across Cultures*, 2nd edn, Prentice Hall, Englewood Cliffs NJ.

Colombia Journal of World Business
Cross Border Acquisitions and Mergers (CSO)
The Economist
Eurostat
The Financial Times
European Journal of Marketing (MCB)
Harvard Business Review
International Journal of Advertising (Blackwell)
International Marketing Review (MCB)
Journal of International Business Studies
Journal of Marketing
Marketing and Research Today (Elsevier)
OECD Publications
Publications of the DTI

Index